Wild about Africa: Sleepwalking on Kilimanjaro and Running from Lions

Alistair McGuinness

Published by Alistair McGuinness, 2020.

WILD ABOUT AFRICA: SLEEPWALKING ON KILIMANJARO AND RUNNING FROM LIONS

First edition. February 24, 2020.

Written by Alistair McGuinness.

Prologue

My first and only close encounter with a spotted hyena occurred unexpectedly in the dark of night. At the time, I was unprepared for such a heart stopping event. Being barefoot didn't help, especially as I was in a remote wooded campsite in the wilds of the Serengeti National Park, Tanzania. I was also dressed for bed, in boxer shorts and a T-shirt. When I say *bed*, I mean a three-season sleeping bag, rolled across the hard floor of a bright orange dome tent.

There were fifteen of us in the camp, including my friend, Owen. Some were support crew of the overland truck we'd joined, but most were travellers from the USA and Europe, all in search of an African adventure. On arrival at the campsite, we'd pitched our tents in a semi-circle around a firepit, which came to life just before sunset.

While sitting around the blazing fire, we tucked into grilled meat and pasta as our tour guide, Michael, handed out drinks, including Tusker beer and chilled wine. After a welcome toast he called for our attention, before quietly explaining that there were no fences to protect us from the nocturnal roaming of predatory animals. Phones were useless without a connection and we had no electricity or running water. All the basics we needed were stored in our truck, now parked up for the night.

After a prompt from one of the passengers, he then changed topic and began sharing a few tales about his life as an overland travel guide. While we sat engrossed, our driver spotted movement at the edge of camp. In the last of the light, we watched a skittish jackal darting between the trees. There were others within the pack, their sandy coats blending with the blood red sky as they circled our camp, lured by the smell of meat.

The sighting of jackals prompted Michael to remind us about stowing all possessions within the tents or on board the truck. He also repeated an earlier message. A pride of lions had recently been spotted in the area, and at the insistence of the Park Ranger we now had an armed guard among us. If needed, his role was to escort us to the rudimentary drop-toilet during the night. This information triggered a flurry of activity for some passengers as they made their way across the open ground towards the makeshift latrine. Once there, they took it in turns to squat over a stinky pit, shielded from view by rough timbers while fending off a swarm of flies!

Three hours later, we were all tucked up safely in our tents, in readiness for a good night's sleep before the early morning game drive. The camp was now silent, except for the snap and crackle of the glowing embers and the gentle snores from a nearby camper. Despite the late hour, I ventured to the tent doorway for one last search of the jackals, opening the zip as wide as I dared to peer outside. Owen was behind me, cocooned in his sleeping bag, torch in one hand, pen in the other, while searching for words to write in his journal. We should have been asleep, but jet lag and a curiosity with the jackals had kept us awake for too long.

The narrow beam from my torch failed to pick any jackals out, as I criss-crossed the open patch of grassland in search of a glint of eyeshine. After a few minutes, I switched off the torch and turned my gaze upwards to enjoy the African night sky, as a warm breeze stirred the branches of a nearby tree.

While searching for constellations amongst the creamy swirl of the Milky Way, a bright streak across the darkened sky called for my attention as a shooting star burst into life. I followed its fiery path, until, in the blink of an eye it burned away, never to return.

I then caught sight of movement by the dwindling fire. At first, I thought it was a mischievous jackal or the armed guard silently escorting someone towards the drop-toilet. But it wasn't a person, unless they'd decided to crawl on all fours. The faint glow from the firelight failed to reveal the identity of the prowler, so I quickly switched on my torch again, expecting to discover a bold jackal. Instead, I caught sight of a menacing creature, with broad shoulders, bone crunching jaws, golden eyes, and a spotted coat.

The hyena was approaching with the stealth of a deadly predator, opening its mouth to reveal a flash of razor-sharp teeth. My heart thumped hard as my mind scrambled to take in the situation. *Fight or flight, fight or flight,* was all I could think of during that moment of terror. But I was barefoot, wearing only boxer shorts and a T-shirt. There was nowhere to run, except to hide in the flimsy two-man tent. In that instant, another thought came to mind.

This must be a dream. This couldn't be happening to me.

A few days earlier, I'd been with Owen at Heathrow Airport, sipping cold beers in the departure lounge while daydreaming about the chance to get up close to African wildlife.

Now it was for real, and this wasn't a dream. I snapped back to reality, noticing within a racing heartbeat that the hyena had taken another step towards me. In my haste, the torch dropped to the ground as I ducked back into the tent and began frantically tugging at the zip handle. My mind scrambled for words, as it refused to budge. And just like the defective zip, my voice had temporarily faltered. I felt a sudden urge to race to the far side of the tent to retrieve my Swiss Army knife, purchased weeks before. According to the shiny label, it had many blades and tools, for every conceivable situation. Would one of them fend off a wolf-sized hyena, on the hunt for a late-night feast?

But I didn't dive for the knife. Instead, I kneeled in the dark, cursing and fretting as I continually yanked on the zip. By now, Owen had scrambled out of his sleeping bag, aware that something was up. He called my name, but my mind was on other things. Any second now, the snarling face of the hyena could appear at the open flap, or worse still, a sharp claw might pierce the thin nylon tent.

Suddenly, the zip started to slide, and I kept the momentum going as the flimsy doorway sealed us from the outside world. Finally, I found my voice. Quiet at first, but louder as the initial shock turned to terror. Owen pointed his torch towards me and in the blinding light my eyes would have looked wide and scary. I scrambled alongside him, screaming over and over. 'HYENA IN THE CAMP–HYENA IN THE CAMP! A MASSIVE ONE–JUST OUTSIDE THE TENT AND THERE MIGHT BE MORE. GUARD, WHERE ARE YOU? GUARD!'

Teenage Dream

"A zebra takes its stripes wherever it goes."
Maasai Proverb

I was 15 years of age when I first caught sight of Mount Kilimanjaro. I still remember studying the herd of zebra standing on the dusty plains of Africa, a snow-clad mountain looming up from the clouds behind them. At the time, I was holding the front cover of a music album, by a British band called The Teardrop Explodes. They'd named the album, *Kilimanjaro*.

Until then, I'd been unaware of the strange-sounding mountain, located a few hundred miles from the equator. I had no idea that a trek to the summit took climbers through five different climate zones, from a hot and steamy jungle to a sub-zero mountaintop, encrusted with snow and ice.

Like many teenagers, I learned a lot about life through music and lyrics, and over the next few months, the tracks on *Kilimanjaro* were played relentlessly, along with my growing collection of eighties sounds. At times, I'd listen while staring out of my bedroom window, wondering what life had in store for me. Eventually, tiny scratches appeared on the vinyl surface of *Kilimanjaro* and for a while it lay forgotten, as other bands fought for my attention.

By the time I was in my mid-twenties, I'd collected a stack of records from musicians that spanned many years and many tastes. I didn't care about trends to follow. I just wanted to sing and dance to songs that had meaning or made me feel alive. Throughout this time, *Kilimanjaro* still made appearances on my turntable. Just as before, I'd listen to the songs while studying the snow-clad mountain on the album cover, wondering if I'd ever get the chance to stand on the African plains and gaze at such a majestic sight.

Home was a friendly, down-to-earth council estate in an industrial town called Luton, 30 miles north of London. Dad lived nearby, but not in the family home. My older siblings had moved out, but I remained at home with Mum, along with my younger brother. Our mum was hard working and selfless. While in her twenties, she'd moved from Ireland to England for the chance of work. This led to love, tears, and laughter, with two marriages, five children, and two divorces along the way. Her children came first and the little money she earned from working at a town centre bakery went into the household.

She wasn't the type to visit the doctors or make a fuss and for this reason her illness went unchecked until it was too late to save her. Unbeknown to family and friends she'd been in constant stomach pain for months. It was during our family holiday to Ireland that the truth emerged. At the time, we were preparing for a family photo on the front lawn. It was the same lawn that she'd often played on as a child, along with her many other brothers and sisters. With expansive views across the hills of Donegal towards the Atlantic Ocean, it had always been a favourite spot to capture special moments during our annual trips.

Just after the photo had been taken, she rushed to the bathroom and called for help from my grandmother and sister. A doctor was called and within a day my mum was back in England, getting tests. While she lay in a hospital bed, I was called to join the rest of my family in a nearby waiting room, where a specialist informed us about her condition. He then quietly explained that the cancer was advanced, with little hope of survival. There wouldn't be any chemotherapy or radiation treatment, as the aggressive tumour had spread too far.

Throughout her brave battle, in and out of hospital, she never once complained as we watched her fade away. During her last months, she stayed at home, mostly in bed. Although her body was weak, she still managed a smile each morning and a few words of encouragement before I headed off to work.

Up until then I'd never heard of the cancer charity called Macmillan, but they soon became part of our family. Like guardian angels, a Macmillan nurse would visit every evening and sit with Mum throughout the night. Eventually, we got to know some of their names. Sometimes she'd smile weakly when they came into her bedroom. 'Hello, Alice, it's Dennis here. Do you remember me? I've come to sit with you for a few hours.'

Other times, she'd sleep while they sat nearby, ever vigilant. During these moments, I'd steal away to play music into the early hours, fighting the anger and grief that surged through me. All her children were by her side, on the night she peacefully passed away.

It took me a few years to figure out the best way to repay the Macmillan nurses. The answer lay on the front cover of my music album, *Kilimanjaro*. By now I was 27, bursting to get out of my hometown and determined to raise money for the charity. A close friend, Owen, was also keen to head to Africa. He was younger than me, quick-witted and popular. Macmillan supplied us with advice and promotional material for getting sponsorship from family and friends, along with a T-shirt each, depicting their logo and name. To earn the pledged money, we had one goal to accomplish:

To trek to the top of Kilimanjaro, 19,340 feet above the plains of Africa!

We also decided to take the plunge and go on a safari before the trek. With no experience in overland travel, we purchased a glossy adventure magazine and studied the advertisements from numerous tour operators. The options ranged in scope and were graded from easy to extreme, including a six-month expedition from the top of

Africa to the bottom. Although appealing, we didn't have the time or budget to pick anything beyond three weeks.

In the end, we chose a two-week overland trip, followed by a week of sunshine on the coast, with the chance to go scuba diving in the Indian Ocean. A package arrived sometime later, filled with detailed information about our upcoming excursion. While reading the names of the places we'd visit, I thought about my mum. She'd have been proud that I was about to embark on a faraway adventure.

I'd heard of some locations on the list, including Nairobi, Mombasa and the Serengeti, but had little idea what to expect in the Ngorongoro Crater. We'd need vaccinations, malaria tablets and three weeks off work. I took the plunge and purchased the most expensive camera I could afford, along with a zoom lens, a new rucksack, suitable clothes for mountaineering and a pair of binoculars.

After touching down in Nairobi, we loaded our luggage onto a trolley and stepped into a crowded arrivals hall. Nearby, I spotted a row of travel kiosks, advertising an array of exciting excursions, including a hot-air balloon flight over the African plains. Colourful posters dotted the walls, highlighting the abundance of wild animals found in the Kenyan game reserves, from majestic lions to vast herds of wildebeest. One poster stood out from the others, portraying graceful giraffes against the backdrop of Mount Kilimanjaro, its snowy peak towering above the sun-baked plains of Amboseli National Park.

At first, we seemed to be the only white faces within view, until the other arrivals from our flight trickled into the hall. I watched as some made their way towards a middle-aged woman, smartly dressed in a pale blue blazer and matching slacks. She stood close to a portable banner, emblazoned with the name of a safari company, and held a clipboard to check off names against the eager tourists gathering round.

We turned our attention to those watching the doorway that led back to passport control and the baggage conveyors. Some held up signs, to attract the attention of those they were collecting. Owen went one way, and I went the other, as we read each sign, hoping to find our names on one of them. Instead, I spent a few awkward moments fending off eager taxi drivers while searching in vain for our pickup.

To escape the hustle, we ventured towards a quiet corner of the hall to gather our thoughts and check our documents. A quick scan revealed that we'd opted out of a private transfer and needed to find our own way to the hotel. After shrugging off this minor mistake, we set our sights on an information console close to the exit. Moments later, a man appeared from the shadows and reached for our trolley. 'Good afternoon and welcome to Kenya. My name is Henry, and my taxi is parked just outside.'

He had a dark chubby face, a bright white smile, and a twinkle in his eyes as he steered the trolley out of the arrivals hall for our first sighting of the African sun. He was keen to talk and strode alongside Owen, his cheerful voice carrying far. 'Are you from England? Do you like Manchester United? They are the best.'

Without waiting for answers, he then changed topic. 'Are you going on safari? I know the best guides and can get you a deal.'

Owen explained that we'd already booked a safari, which he accepted with a smile before pointing towards a row of parked cars. 'This way please–my taxi is nearby.'

Somewhere in my luggage I'd packed a wide-brimmed hat and sunglasses, but Henry didn't hear my call as he expertly steered our trolley past a row of parked cars hugging the verge of the pickup point. Newly arrived passengers struggled with luggage, while men in uniforms blew whistles and tried keeping the traffic moving. As we crossed over the road, it soon became clear that his car wasn't *just* outside but in the middle of a neighbouring car park. Owen followed closely while I detoured towards an outdoor kiosk for three bottles of water. By the time I caught up with them, I'd already glugged half my share. By now, they'd stashed the luggage in the boot of Henry's clean but road-weary taxi.

While Henry and Owen sat side by side in the front, I lounged in the back, enjoying the tropical sun as it warmed my face. We'd jetted away from a washed-out English summer, where the sun had hardly made an appearance. Now, it was impossible to miss, high in the sky, without a cloud in sight.

As we approached the centre of Nairobi, I studied the scene outside. Just like any other big cities, there were half-finished high rises, roads jammed with cars and street sellers hustling for business. I could have been in any large city, except for one giveaway: walking towards us was a young man, dressed in a bright red shawl and sandals. He had jet black skin, lean features, braided hair and carried a wooden staff. I knew about the Maasai, one of Kenya's oldest tribes, but hadn't expected to see a tribesman in traditional clothing on the busy streets of Nairobi.

We watched as he came to a crossing, standing tall and proud while looming over the head of a middle-aged businessman, squeezed into a grey suit. As they passed in front of us, I noticed a signpost pointing towards Nairobi National Park, which triggered a response from Henry as he studied me in the rear-view mirror. 'Would you like to visit the park? I can take you now, or later?' He then turned in his seat, his eyes wide as he smiled and said, 'It is a special place that is often overlooked by tourists. Where else can you find wild lions, so close to a city centre?'

Although appealing, we were due to head off in the morning on a weeklong safari. After the long-haul flight from England, the lure of a warm shower and an ice-cold beer was all I craved. As for spotting lions in the African bush, hopefully we'd get our chance later in the week!

We appreciated Henry's gesture but dismissed the offer, which he shrugged off easily before turning his attention to the car radio. As the next song began to play, he lowered the volume and said, 'This song is called, *Jambo Bwana* and is perfect for learning a few Swahili greetings. Please listen and I will teach you.'

He then turned the dial and sang along with the next words. '*Jambo, jambo bwana, habari garni, mzuri sana.*'

While the song continued, he called out, '*Jambo,* means hello, and *jambo bwana,* means hello sir.'

After a nod from Owen, he continued with the explanations. '*Habari garni,* means how are you, and *mzuri sana*, means I am fine.'

Throughout the song, he continued line by line, happily converting each Swahili phrase into English. After the song had finished, Henry shared a few more helpful expressions, including *asante sana,* which means, thank you. He continued with the friendly banter as we navigated the streets and slowed by our budget hotel to allow a barrier to be raised, manned by a security guard. As we drove past the guard toward a compact parking lot, Henry said, 'It is just a precaution, to keep the tourists safe.'

While he helped with our luggage, Owen rummaged for a worthy tip. After stowing the money, Henry shook our hands before offering some advice. 'I hope you enjoy your stay in Nairobi. Beware at night-time, as sometimes the streets are wilder than the game parks. If you need a lift at any time, here is my card.'

As he pulled away, Owen called out, 'Asante sana.'

In reply, he waved and said, 'Hakuna matata,' before threading his way into the downtown traffic.

As we entered the bright and breezy foyer, I heard a familiar pop song playing from an overhead speaker. While we checked into our rooms, I smiled at the receptionist and hummed the first words to the catchy tune:

Jambo
Jambo Bwana
Habari Garni
Mzuri Sana

That afternoon, we met up with the others who'd signed up for the same African adventure. During sundowners by the pool, we shared names and spoke about the places we called home. With only one night in Nairobi, we were keen to get out of the hotel and knew just the man to call. Henry drove us to a carvery called Carnivore, located away from the city centre. Along the way, he slowed alongside nightclubs and bars, but we were not in the mood for late-night antics. Instead, we urged him to keep to the plan, as the day had been long enough already. He dropped us off by the entrance, with a promise to stay close for whenever we called. The door to the restaurant was opened by a man in a white uniform, smiling as he ushered us inside. 'Good evening to you both, and welcome to Carnivore ...'

We soon discovered that each diner is given an inch high flag upon arrival, made from colourful card, emblazoned with the logo of the restaurant. Once seated, the customers are encouraged to fly their flags by placing them in designated holders found on each table. This is a signal for the waiting staff to continually return with offers of charcoal roasted meats, including crocodile and ostrich, plus the traditional favourites of lamb and beef. After an hour, we lowered our flags, paid the bill, and tipped our waiter.

We then ventured to the beer garden, to enjoy cold beers while seated by the warmth of a fire. There were other tourists around the firepit, each with a story to tell about their adventures in Kenya. We overheard snippets from a couple that had recently enjoyed a sunrise safari with a difference. During their balloon flight, they'd spotted lions on the hunt and had been treated to a champagne breakfast upon landing in the bush. Although we were keen to listen to more fireside stories, an early start was planned for our departure to the Tanzanian border.

Luckily, Henry was waiting nearby to drop us off at the hotel. Along the way, he detoured towards another lively strip, filled with bars and cafes. Between yawns, we told him to speed up in case we changed our minds! The following morning, we ventured to the restaurant for a hearty breakfast to sustain us during the trip to the border.

The overland bus trip from Nairobi to Tanzania didn't go smoothly. I guess that's Africa for you. There is always something unpredictable waiting to happen and this was to be our first mishap of the journey. The town of Namanga is located on the border between Kenya and Tanzania and is one of the main entry and exit points between the two countries. Such places always attract a variety of characters. Some, like Owen and myself, were wide-eyed as we approached the outskirts of town. A day earlier, we'd been sipping beers at 35,000 feet, daydreaming about spotting wildlife and touching the snows of Kilimanjaro.

Now we were dressed in sweaty singlets and shorts, sitting side by side in a cramped minibus while listening to instructions from our driver about what to expect at the border. Above the rattle of the diesel engine and shrill of the cooling fan, I heard him mention money changers and exchange rates. I should have listened further but was far too interested in the passing street life.

The sides of our vehicle were covered in a sheen of red dirt, churned up by the wheels, so I slid the nearest window open to get a better view. There were people everywhere. Some were on bikes while others walked slowly alongside the road, where wooden stalls were laden with fruit and vegetables. Shops ranged in size from tin shacks to single-storey buildings, constructed from rough brick or cement. Some looked to be abandoned, but others were open for business. What they sold or did, I had no idea.

There were few shoppers, despite the colourful advertisements stuck to the sides of tin walls or roofs. Coca-Cola signs were a common sight, their red and white branding strategically positioned above shop fronts. A billboard of a fashionable black woman with a pearly smile and wearing bright white clothes caught my attention; she was holding aloft a packet of OMO washing powder.

I spotted a man dressed in a suit and tie, standing by a tree and watching from afar, but he didn't return my wave. Further on, I saw a woman squatting beside the road, with oranges to sell. She'd stacked them three high, into the shape of a pyramid to catch the eye of passers-by. At an intersection, I stared down a narrow road and caught sight of two men in military uniform, holding wooden batons while pointing to a group of youths. The bus lurched forward, and the moment was gone.

The antiquated truck directly in front of our minibus continually spewed diesel fumes from a blackened exhaust. The red Toyota behind was filled with passengers, each singing along to the pulsating music blasting through their open windows. Our driver dropped another gear and suddenly we were travelling at the same pace as the pedestrians.

I poked my camera lens out of the open window to get a photo of a dog scavenging by the roadside. Then I spotted a man, trotting towards our minibus. He was smiling widely and began waving. 'Hey, mister, you want Tanzanian shillings? I will give you the best price.'

He was tall, with a long gait that kept up easily with our diminishing speed. I declined the offer and snapped the window shut, just as our driver called out again. 'We are about to arrive at the Tanzanian border. Please make sure your passports are ready. Once they have been stamped, head to the exit to meet your overland guide. His name is Michael and he'll escort you to the truck, in readiness for your safari and Kilimanjaro climb.'

After stopping the minibus, the driver stepped into the narrow aisle and called for our attention. 'Here is the warning once more, in case you didn't hear the first time or were too busy taking photos of stray dogs. By the way, in the days ahead, there will be far more exciting animals to take photos of. Like I said earlier, don't exchange money at the border with anyone. Your guide is the best person to advise you. I am a proud African, but you must appreciate that some of these locals will do their best to get you to part with your money! Please be careful and above all, I hope you have an amazing holiday.'

We stepped out of the vehicle, loaded down with our rucksacks, and were directed towards passport control. Despite the prickly heat, the atmosphere inside seemed relaxed as seated officials called us forward one by one, to complete the arrivals process. Owen went before me and got his passport stamped without delay. I was then called forward to take his place.

The official kept a stern face as he reached out to take my passport from the counter. While flicking through the pages, he looked up briefly, his eyes on mine for a split second, before he turned his attention to a keyboard and started tapping. After a quick scan of a computer screen, he then asked why I was visiting Tanzania. I felt a sense of excitement while spilling the news about the camping safari and Kilimanjaro climb.

It was nothing new. He'd heard it all a thousand times before, from eager travellers arriving from across the world. He then made a show of comparing my jaded face to the passport photo before him. Seemingly happy, he then asked, 'Alistair, have you been to Tanzania before?'

For a fleeting moment, my heart missed a beat. Was I on some type of Interpol report? Then I realised it was just a standard question, asked routinely throughout his long shift on border patrol. I eased out a smile, convincing him of my innocence. 'No, it's my first time, but the people seem to be really friendly.'

In response, I heard the satisfying thud of his ink pad as he stamped one of the empty pages within my passport. He handed me the travel document and acknowledged my thanks with a slight nod of the head. 'I hope you enjoy your stay Mister McGuinness. I'm afraid we don't all get the chance to climb Kilimanjaro. I hear you must walk slowly and drink lots of water. Good luck, sir.'

He then turned his attention to the next in line as I strolled away from passport control, into Tanzania. Just outside the building, I found Owen, in deep discussion with a stranger. I ambled over, smiling widely at the thought that our adventure was finally taking shape. The man talking with Owen was at least six feet tall, with a few days of growth protruding from a lean jaw. His black skin glistened lightly with sweat, but his smile was cool, calm, and collected. Owen turned towards me and said, 'Ali, this is our driver. His name is George.'

George looked down at me and smiled, before reaching to pick up Owen's rucksack. In one swift motion, he placed it onto his head and balanced the heavy load with a steady hand. He then pointed away from the building and said quietly, 'Follow me, please. I will take you to the truck.'

Within seconds, he'd joined a mass of pedestrians, and Owen was close behind. I'd only taken a few steps when I heard my name being called. It was John, a retired marine veteran, on holiday from the USA. We'd shared beers with him at our hotel in Nairobi and he'd sat in the front of our minibus, all the way to Namanga. He was standing alongside a wide-shouldered man, with short mousey hair, a deep tan and the beginnings of a beard. The man wore a green cotton shirt, emblazoned with the same logo that I'd seen on the information pack that came through the post, months earlier.

For a split second, I was unsure what to do. Stay close to Owen or shake hands with the representative from our travel company. John made the decision for me and called out again. 'Hey Alistair, this is Michael. He's going to be our guide for the safari.'

I didn't want to be impolite, but my thoughts were on Owen, so after a quick handshake I enquired about George, our driver. Michael's eyes narrowed as he said, 'I'm sorry, mate, but I've no idea what you're talking about. There's no one called George in my team.'

He sounded like a Kiwi, but I didn't have the time to ask. My mind was on Owen, as I'd finally realised that he was heading in totally the wrong direction, with the wrong type of person. I tried explaining my dilemma as fast as possible, the words spilling out. 'My friend has just gone off, with a man who claimed to be our driver. He said his name was George and—'

Michael cut me short, his voice raised. 'Are you kidding me? Didn't you listen to the advice on the minibus?'

Instead of waiting for an answer, he continued with his spiel. 'My driver is waiting in the truck. If your friend is with a tout, he could soon be in trouble. Which way did he go?'

I pointed out Owen's red rucksack, perched on George's head, far in the distance. Considering that I'd convinced him to come to Africa, I felt a sense of responsibility and set off in pursuit. I then heard Michael shout out, his words competing with the tooting of car horns. 'Wait up. I'm coming with you. Don't change any money, whatever you do.'

Without looking back, I called out, 'Okay, I won't. I promise.'

I kept my eyes on Owen's rucksack while weaving through a crowd of pedestrians. It didn't help that I was carting a heavy pack, and with every stride, my shoulders protested as the straps dug in. I heard voices calling out to me but ignored the distractions to concentrate on Owen's rucksack, which stood out like a beacon against a sea of black faces. Then suddenly, it was gone!

I arrived at a junction and stood panting, while looking around for signs of Owen and George. To my right, the road narrowed into an alleyway, where a group of men watched me with interest. Instinctively, I turned left, away from the onlookers and into a courtyard, surrounded by run-down shops and a scattering of empty market stalls.

I spotted them at once, standing in the shade of a tree, outside a disused butcher's shop. There was no one else around, and Owen was still smiling. George was holding a wad of Tanzanian shillings, which were then peeled back one by one, as he began counting the money. Considering the short distance that I'd run, my breathing felt ragged as I yelled a warning. 'Owen, this isn't our driver. We need to go.'

George stared at me from across the courtyard, still maintaining a wide, bright smile. 'Don't worry, bwana. I'll take you to your truck soon enough. I just need to do a little business with your friend and will give him a good deal.'

Despite my protest, they exchanged money and sealed the deal with a handshake, both seemingly content with the transaction. At this stage, I should have prodded Owen into action, as we needed to make haste. Instead, George turned his attention to me and took a few steps closer. 'What about you, my friend? I have a few shillings left and as a special promotion will do the same deal.'

I glanced at Owen, and he nodded slightly. While reaching for my money belt, I heard nearby voices and snapped back to reality. What had I been thinking? I spotted a group of youths, standing in the shadows, watching with interest as Owen stashed away his cash. I gestured for him to join me and tried sounding confident, despite the tight knots forming in my stomach. 'Well, it looks like everyone is happy now. Owen, let's go. We need to find the truck.'

Just as we turned to leave, I heard heavy footsteps approaching. A man burst into the courtyard, panting for breath. It was Michael, and he didn't look happy! He pointed towards us and called out, 'Okay, let's get you two out of here. Didn't you get a briefing on the bus? Don't come complaining to me later, when you realise you've been scammed.'

While he gave us a dressing down, George strolled away without a word, and by the time we were back in the main street, he was nowhere to be seen. Michael then led us towards our overland truck. Along the way, he collected the remaining passengers, who were waiting patiently by the customs building.

As we stood in a half circle alongside the sturdy vehicle, he briefly explained about the dangers of changing money with strangers. This included robbery, receiving fake notes, getting cheated on conversion rates and also picking up a heavy fine by the police, for illegal practises. He'd done a quick calculation of Owen's backstreet transaction and was happy to inform us he'd been let off lightly because of the small amount traded between them.

He then changed topic and introduced us to one of the most important people on our tour. Peter was tall and black, with a beaming smile and rounded belly. He would be our driver for the next seven days and knew most roads like the back of his hand, with many years of experience behind the wheel.

Michael then shared a few details about himself. As I'd guessed, he was a Kiwi. He'd been away from New Zealand for a few years and had guided many trips across Africa. He was 35 and had travelled to over 40 countries, with three successful attempts at climbing Kilimanjaro.

He then turned his attention to our Mercedes truck and pointed out the key features, including the cooking equipment and storage system. He didn't think we'd be getting bogged, but if needed, we had all the gear on board to free us from most sticky situations. While we explored our new surroundings, he explained that everything in the truck had a home, with expectations to keep it that way. When it came to cooking, cleaning and preparing food, we'd all be part of a rotation system, but there would also be plenty of free time.

Most seats had compartments underneath them, where a cache of tinned food sat ready to save the day if rations fell low. Previous overlanders had donated unused items, including tea, coffee, spices and cooking oil. By the end of our trip, we were expected to do the same.

Plans were also in place to climb Kilimanjaro, but not before the chance to go on safari. We were a mixed bunch, spanning 30 years and many homelands, including the USA, Britain and Germany. Some, like John, had travelled much of the world, while others, like me and Owen, had rarely ventured overseas.

After climbing on board, we settled into our seats, to prepare for the half-day drive towards Ngorongoro Crater, a UNESCO World Heritage Site. The ten-mile-wide crater was formed over two million years ago, after the cone of an active volcano imploded, following a massive eruption. Scientists call the phenomenon a *caldera*, and this one, in the heart of East Africa, has evolved into a wildlife haven.

At first, we watched from the open windows of the truck, hoping to spot wildlife, but with each hour it became clear that any sightings would be rare outside of the game parks. Instead, we gazed at the wide-open skies and drove along a gravel road; the tyres kicking up red dirt as the sun beat down on faraway hills.

Into the Wild

"Light a campfire and everyone's a storyteller."
John Geddes

We stayed overnight in a simple lodge, a few kilometres from the crater rim, and were woken just before daylight. During breakfast, we were split into groups, in readiness to head into the crater in open-topped Land Rovers. Despite the alluring smell of grilled bacon and fresh coffee wafting across the dining room, there was little time for second portions. The drivers were waiting, and the rising sun had already displaced the morning chill.

At the lip of the crater, we stopped briefly for a photo opportunity. John was sitting in the front passenger seat, his camera clicking as he tried to capture the moment. He then turned to the driver and said, 'Oh man, this is the Africa I dreamed of as a kid.'

Before us lay a natural sanctuary for thousands of wild animals. A vast soda lake shimmered in the early light, surrounded by grassland. A bloated cloud, low and menacing, cast a single shadow onto the crater floor, promising the chance of an early shower. The cloud inched across the wide sky, and I watched its shadow move silently towards the lake.

It was only when the driver switched off the diesel engine that the absolute stillness hit us. For a few precious moments, no one spoke. There was no need to, as the landscape before us was doing all the talking. One passenger used the time to survey the crater floor, using powerful binoculars that she'd pulled from a personal daypack. I watched her smile, and then heard her voice, animated at first and then whisper quiet. 'Is that a zebra? Yes, I'm sure. There's another, and another.'

Then she began muttering to herself in German, as she slowly scanned the crater floor. When she spoke next, the words were once again in English, but loud enough for us all to hear. 'I think I can see an elephant. Wait, there are two more and one has tusks.'

Those without binoculars turned their attention to the driver, and within moments, we were heading down a gravel track, towards the crater floor. The convoy split up as soon as the land levelled out, and with the whole day to explore, we went in search of wildlife.

There are believed to be 25,000 animals in the crater and from what I could see during the first few hours, most were of the hoofed variety. Zebras and wildebeest were common sights throughout the morning and soon became as familiar as double-decker buses on the streets of London. In drier sections, fine dust clouds gave away the position of other vehicles, as they crossed the crater floor in search of elusive animals.

It was John that spotted the black rhino, far in the distance, standing proud against the steep sides of the crater rim. Our driver gave the animal the space it deserved and stopped the engine from 30 metres away. In the silence that followed, we jostled for elbow-room, cameras poised, for a close-up of its priceless horn. The solitude didn't last for long. Another vehicle appeared at our side, followed shortly after by three more. I tried counting the number of zoom lenses pointing towards the critically endangered creature, but lost interest after reaching ten.

Although the rhino seemed undisturbed by the half circle of vehicles nearby, our driver didn't look as relaxed. I could hear his mutterings and leaned in close, to listen further. 'We've reached the maximum number of vehicles that are allowed near an animal. But I think five is too many, especially for the rhinos.'

He noticed another Land Rover, parked close to a tree, as if waiting for a vacant slot. Then he said, 'Okay, it's time to go. I hope you've all had time to take photos.'

During lunch by the lake, we ducked low to avoid swooping birds, which were in search of easy pickings. Some flew so close that you could feel the rush of air as they tried to pluck the food from our hands. As we prepared for an afternoon drive, our guide explained some of the challenges facing the wildlife, including poaching. He also shared that very few animals venture out of the crater, even though the vast plains of the Serengeti are relatively close by. Lions are vulnerable to in-breeding, because of a diminishing gene pool, caused in part by human encroachment. There is also the daily intrusion from those on safari, including vehicle noise and disturbance to bush tracks.

By the time we resumed the game drive, the air had become hot and still. Hours later, bathed in sweat and low on water, I began thinking about the ice-cold beer, waiting for me at the lodge bar. One passenger decided on a mid-afternoon nap, but John remained vigilant, sitting upright as he scanned the terrain. Without him, we wouldn't have had the chance to enjoy the leopard, resting along the limb of an acacia tree. As the sun began to drop, our luck continued, with a faraway glimpse of a large buffalo crossing a stream, followed soon after by the sighting of a bull elephant, emerging from a scattering of trees.

As we headed towards the crater rim, the driver slowed the vehicle and pointed towards a patch of tall grass. The sun had turned the grass a golden brown, and we had to concentrate hard to spot the lioness, watching our every move from afar. As soon as we stopped the vehicle, she stood up, and then swished her tail, as if in irritation at being found. She then turned away and walked towards the setting sun. Within seconds, there was no trace of her.

That evening, while enjoying drinks at the lodge, I sat alongside the other passengers as we chatted about our day in the crater. I felt as though I'd seen more wild animals in one day, than I had in a lifetime. One passenger reminded us all that we'd been lucky enough to spot the *Big Five*, which are rhino, leopard, elephant, buffalo, and lion.

Hunters first used the "Big Five" term during colonial times, to refer to the most dangerous and popular animals to pursue on foot. Although hunting is now banned in most African game reserves, the term is still used, particularly as a promotional reference to attract visitors. As Owen handed me another beer, I thought back to our time in the crater. I clinked glasses and raised mine high, wondering about the unique location we'd just experienced.

The crater is not only home to threatened wildlife but also a location where humans and animals coexist. The Maasai still practice traditional livestock grazing within the crater, but their way of life is under pressure. Like many indigenous tribes across the world, loss of habitat, an erosion of culture and the spread of urbanisation has affected their way of life. Traditionally, they've herded cattle, goats and sheep, and when possible, move with the seasons to ensure their families and livestock have access to fresh water. Their villages are known as *kraals*, with each house constructed from mud, grass, cow dung and sticks.

As the night came to an end, I enquired about the nearest Maasai village and was assured by the receptionist that there were a few within the vicinity. With this thought in mind, I ambled back to the tent with Owen, our torchlights probing the darkness for any nocturnal creatures that may have found a gap in the perimeter fence!

We were given a few hours grace the following morning, to enjoy the camp pool and a cooked breakfast. We'd been seated alongside the other passengers, which gave us the time to chat about our next destination. John had his guidebook open and pointed towards a map of the Serengeti, which included the location of the campsite we'd be staying in. It looked to be far from any roads, with few creature comforts.

He began to read aloud, so those nearby could learn more about the vastness of the Serengeti and its proximity to the game reserves of southern Kenya. While he merrily chatted away, I sipped my coffee and studied the chalets surrounding the pool, each with a toilet, shower, and a comfortable bed. I'd heard that many game parks had similar types of lodges, with five-star amenities on offer to those that could afford them. But for now, I didn't envy their luxury. I felt ready for the simple comforts of an open fire, a cosy tent and the closeness to nature.

By the time we made our way to the truck, the sun was showing its strength. Peter informed us that the drive would take about four hours, including a stop for lunch. Our aim was to be set up at the campsite by sunset. By luck, I managed to sit alongside Owen and Beryl in the outside seats, positioned above the driver's cab. They offered uninterrupted views of the gravel road and the gentle contours of faraway hills.

Within the first hour, Beryl spotted a Maasai village, close to a selection of trees. As we drew closer, two men appeared from the scrub and waved us down. They were tall and slim and wore red shawls, known as *shukas*, across strong shoulders. The truck pulled over to the verge, and Michael jumped out first. He then called out, 'Guys, if you want to visit a Maasai village, then this is your chance. Please remember to show some respect, especially if you want to take photos.'

We clambered down from the truck and followed the two men across the coarse grass towards their village. They walked with a natural gait, taking large strides, as we followed close behind. During the walk towards the first hut, we passed a ringed fence, constructed from the thorny branches of an acacia tree. A scrawny goat lay down inside the enclosure, its yellow eyes watching our arrival with interest.

Two young women approached, smiling widely as they held out woven baskets filled with colourful beadwork and bracelets. Their hair had been shaved close to the scalp and both wore cotton dresses, partly covered by red shawls. Their long and colourful earrings had stretched the holes in each earlobe, causing them to elongate. Beryl and a few others were soon exchanging dollars for trinkets.

John made a point of showing the men his camera, to which they nodded and smiled. After he'd taken a few quick snaps, they ushered him towards the women who were selling bracelets. I was more intrigued by their homes than the items for sale and walked over to another hut. Without prompting, I was led inside by one of the men. Unusually for me, I had to duck my head when entering the doorway.

Apart from discarded blankets, there was little else to see, but it instantly felt cooler than the oppressive heat outside. Elongated slits had been cut into the walls, to offer light and an escape route for whenever a fire was lit. The matted roof felt sturdy to touch, with no apparent gaps. The faint smell of wood smoke and cattle dung caught at my throat, triggering a series of coughs as I made my way outside.

From the edge of the village, another man appeared, dragging branches towards the animal enclosure. He looked to be in his early thirties, with long red hair, braided with beads. He also wore a shuka and held a short sword, known as a *seme*. As he began hacking at the branches, I decided to venture nearer. He didn't seem to mind and continued with his work, while I stood nearby, trying to absorb the sights and sounds.

Moments earlier, I'd been on top of the truck, sitting alongside Beryl, while sharing jokes. Now she was trying on handcrafted jewellery, and I was considering the fate of the trussed-up goat. We weren't the first overlanders to visit the village, but the lack of goods for sale and their bright smiles helped create a relaxed atmosphere.

Already, most of the group were heading back to the truck and I heard the guide call my name. I wanted to take a photo of the man as he worked, but didn't want to spoil the moment. He stopped and offered me the short sword, then made a gesture for me to hack at the dried branches.

My attempts were met by bouts of hearty laughter from the men and soft giggles from the women. Then I heard my name being called again. It was time to go. Instead of handing back the tool, I decided it was my time to barter. I traded a wind-up torch along with some Tanzanian shillings and ran back to the truck, holding the short sword aloft.

After we waved the villagers goodbye, I studied my memento. It was light, with a double-edged steel blade, protected by a red-dyed leather sheath. John was seated nearby and I watched as he opened his guidebook while calling for attention. Over the rattle of the engine, I strained to listen as he read a passage out loud. 'It says here that the Maasai people favour bold red colours, as it symbolises courage, bravery and strength. They also believe that the colour scares off predators.'

Feeling thankful for my hand-crafted memento, I stored it carefully in my daypack and returned my gaze to the open road, hoping to find something of interest before Beryl did! While the sun crept across the sky, the truck continued its journey. Some passengers played cards, others dozed and a few scribbled lines into travel diaries, despite the rattles and bumps resonating through the suspension.

Suddenly, giraffes were spotted between the trees, causing a flurry of excitement. As we approached the Serengeti, wildlife sightings increased further, including skittish zebra and nervous warthogs, their tails erect as they scurried away. Someone pointed to fresh dollops of elephant dung, scattered across a dried riverbed, which caused one or two passengers to get their cameras ready.

Now, as we neared the game park, the passengers came to life, each of us peering outside for further signs of wildlife. The official entrance to the Serengeti consisted of a rough stone wall, set back from the road. It was crowned with the weathered skull of an antelope, its spiral horns prominent against a cobalt sky. Peter parked nearby and cut the engine. While he ambled towards a small brick complex to complete some paperwork, we stepped down from the truck, into bright sunshine.

Most passengers hunted for shade or went in search of water. I decided to stretch my legs and explore the compound. There wasn't much to see, apart from a pile of discarded bricks by a wire fence. I stepped over the wire and moved away from the compound, drawn to the faraway sight of a dust devil, whipping dirt into the air. By now, I'd been joined by a cloud of flies, but their constant buzzing paled into insignificance at the sight of the endless plains spread out before me. Far in the distance, where the land and sky touched, a heat haze shimmered.

Nothing in the itinerary had prepared me for the way I felt at that very moment. Here I was, on an African adventure. Not a six-month major expedition, but an adventure all the same. More importantly, I was half a world away from my normal life, back home. Out there, beyond the horizon, was a world I knew very little about, except for snippets that I'd learned by watching wildlife documentaries from the comfort of my sofa. But there was no remote control to switch channels, if I decided to change my mind. Suddenly, it all felt very real.

I thought back to my mum and wondered how she would have felt in such a location. She'd mostly holidayed in the place of her birth, in the northwest of Ireland, with friends and family. As a child, I'd gone there every year during summer holidays and had grown fond of the annual pilgrimage. County Donegal, with its misty hills, wild coastline, lively music, and warm-hearted people, had made an impression on all her children. I finally felt ready to experience somewhere new and what better location could there be, than the Serengeti.

Its name is derived from the Maasai term, meaning 'endless plains.' The undulating grassland occasionally gives way to woodland, lakes and rivers, all of which are home to many species of wildlife. Of these, it is the annual migration spectacle, involving millions of hoofed animals, that captures the imagination. Vast herds of wildebeest, along with thousands of zebra and gazelle, move through the park each year, in search of lush grazing and water.

During their passage through Kenya and Tanzania, they are continually stalked. Big cats hunt them on land, and at migratory river crossings, crocodiles wait patiently in channels of water. If they get the chance, they strike with speed and ferocity. Lions thrive in the Serengeti and for good reason, mainly due to the abundance of food and the wide-open spaces. With an estimated population of 3,000 lions, the Serengeti must be one of the best places in the world to spot them.

I was buzzing with excitement at the thought of a sunrise safari, followed days later by the chance to raise money for Macmillan by climbing Mount Kilimanjaro. Many friends, family and work colleagues–hundreds of people in total–had pledged money for the charity and we'd even packed Macmillan T-shirts, which we planned to wear on the summit.

Convincing Owen to climb Kilimanjaro rather than partake in a beachside holiday had been a minor challenge, but he was fully embracing the adventure so far. On any normal Friday we'd have been preparing for a night on the town, but that world of normality was on hold, especially as the nearest sizeable town was over 300 kilometres away.

After returning to the compound, I caught sight of Owen kneeling alongside a brick wall. I soon discovered that he was studying a speckled lizard, basking in the sunshine. While we tried taking photos, a man appeared from the building, dressed smartly in a khaki top, with matching shorts and walking boots. He gave a friendly wave towards the newcomers while walking purposefully towards Michael. 'Good afternoon, bwana. Welcome back. How was the drive today?'

Michael reached for the man's outstretched hand and said, 'The road was a little bumpy in places, but I'm excited to be back in the Serengeti.'

'Yes, I'm sure. We had a few showers last week, but the sun is finally out, so the tracks should be fine for your truck. Now, I have some news for you. Have you heard about the lions?'

The mention of lions hushed the group, and while he spoke with Michael, we hung on to his every word. 'There have been reports that a pride has been visiting the camping spot you're booked into. A few days ago, a male lion decided to take a midnight nap against the side of a two-man tent. The occupants remained inside but were a little shaken the next morning. Due to the unusual behaviour and increased sightings, I'm insisting you take an armed guard during your stay.'

He then pointed towards a nearby tree, where a man wearing a red beret squatted patiently. 'You need to hire this man for the next few days. He is from one of the local tribes and will be your guard.'

Michael glanced over at the guard and shook his head in annoyance. 'But I've been taking groups into the Serengeti for years and have never needed an armed escort before.'

The ranger had the last word. 'These are the new rules. No doubt they will change, but for now you must have a guard.'

As if on cue, Peter appeared from the building and signalled that it was time to go. The armed guard in question looked to be in his early twenties, with lean features and wiry limbs, hidden under a faded camouflage uniform. After a hasty introduction by Michael, he stepped on board without a word, and then stood by the open doorway.

After we'd pulled away from the park entrance, he caught me staring at his rifle and gave a flashing smile before reaching for his water bottle. As the wheels bounced across the pitted track, the engine roared, causing me to raise my voice to be heard. 'Are there many lions in the area at the moment?'

His smile widened as he eyed me up and down. He was holding the rifle with one hand, its stock resting on the floor, with the barrel angled towards the open doorway. By now, every passenger was watching as he leaned close to me and said, 'Don't worry, bwana. You look too skinny for the lions of the Serengeti. They need plenty of meat and will leave you alone, I'm sure.'

He'd gained our attention and raised his voice a little more. 'There is a basic toilet in the camp, and I suggest you use it before going to sleep. If you need to visit it after dark, don't venture outside alone. Call out for me and I will escort you. If I don't respond, it means that the lions were very hungry tonight!'

He started to laugh, just as our driver spotted a herd of zebra crossing the track. We slowed to let them continue their journey, our cameras clicking to capture a real life, Zebra Crossing. Two hours later, we came to a complete stop, alongside a row of trees. While we set up the tents, prepared the fire and collectively organised dinner, the setting sun cast our long shadows across the open plains. A few days earlier, we'd flown from various parts of the world, daydreaming about an African adventure. Now we were deep in the Serengeti, watching faraway clouds turn pink, while nearby, our armed guard stood quietly with a mug of coffee.

As we sat by the fire, Michael passed around barbequed ribs and briefed us about the next few days. We'd timed our arrival with the annual migration of wildebeest and were sure to spot hundreds, if not thousands of them. As for our simple camp, in his opinion it was one of the best places to stay in Tanzania, with no added extras needed. There were no fences to protect us from the wildlife, which meant staying in our tents all night. We weren't to wander from camp, were likely to hear lions prowling in the night, and would begin the first safari drive at dawn.

If we needed to use the drop-toilet, the best advice was to go now or hang on until daylight. If desperate, we could call out for an armed escort. In the last of the light, we spotted dark shapes in the distance, skulking between bushes and trees as a pack of jackals skirted the fringes of our camp. I was searching the foreground with the binoculars I'd purchased weeks before, when the guard tapped me on the shoulder. 'Bwana, the jackals are afraid of the fire, but will scavenge the camp while you are fast asleep. It is not them you have to worry about.'

With that, he went in search of more coffee and I lowered the binoculars to study the evening sky. The sun was directly behind an acacia tree and seemed to have bloated during its plunge to the horizon. It was now a hazy red ball, inching lower as the clouds above burst into life, turning crimson pink against the darkening sky. By the time I resumed my search with the binoculars, the jackals had vanished, swallowed up by the night.

After our meal, we sat around the campfire. Some passengers chatted quietly together, while others stared up at the night sky, in search of shooting stars. Owen was proving to be a popular character within our diverse group. He'd been blessed with dark hair, olive skin, a charming smile and the warm personality to complement such features. I could see him now, silhouetted by the firelight, chatting with John, the Vietnam veteran. Alongside was Beryl, a mild-mannered, middle-aged woman from England, who was travelling alone. She was good-humoured, mildly flirtatious and had trained hard for the Kilimanjaro trek. When probed, she gave very little away about her life in England, except to say she was looking forward, not backward.

Apart from John, there were two other Americans in our group. Chris and Steve were in their late twenties and had been friends for years. They were both chatty, with a range of interests, from politics to sport. Since our meeting in Nairobi, Chris had talked openly about the strict training regime they'd followed, to ensure they were fit enough for the Kilimanjaro challenge. Further discussions revealed they'd both graduated from university with first class honours, and now worked in the corporate world. Chris had blonde hair, tightly curled and cut short, while his friend opted for the surfer look, with dark hair that brushed against wide shoulders.

In contrast to their strict training regime, Owen and I had been more relaxed. We'd recently been on a walking weekend in the Lake District, covering 20 miles on the first day and 15 on the second. With no blisters to report, despite the rocky outcrops and steep hills, we figured that Owen's youthful vigour and my gritty determination would get us to the frozen summit of Kilimanjaro.

One by one, the travellers stood up by the dwindling fire, made their excuses and prepared for bed. Some, like Beryl, took up the offer of an armed escort to the long-drop toilet. It was basically a narrow hole in the earth, screened by wooden sides, with a simple lock on the door. I'd made a visit before sunset, dry retching while my bowels emptied into the deep pit, my hands windmilling to keep a swarm of flies away from my exposed buttocks.

Sometime later, the camp was in silence, except for the sharp crackles from our firepit as the embers settled. The only other sound was the soft tap of pen on paper, as Owen scribbled words into his journal by torchlight. Suddenly, he stopped writing and pointed his torch towards the tent flap. 'Did you hear that, Ali?'

I lifted my head from the travel pillow and tuned into the night sounds. Apart from the persistent call of a cricket, I heard a hoarse cough somewhere in the distance and smiled at the gentle snores resonating from our war veteran. I felt compelled to whisper, even though the night was still comparatively young. 'It's John snoring I reckon, and I think the guard has a persistent cough. I'll just take one more look outside, as we've got an early start in the morning.'

Moments later, I was screaming for the armed guard!

Thick as Thieves

"Everyone wants to eat, but few are willing to hunt."
Unknown

Despite my frantic calls, the guard never appeared and nobody else stirred. Although we could see the haze of my torchlight through the thin nylon of the tent, none of us dare move. We left the torch where it lay and silently returned to our sleeping bags, fearful that any noise would tempt the hyena to return.

Soon after, we drifted off to sleep, lulled by the sound of crickets. Although exhausted, I should have slept through the night, but I woke with a jolt and opened my eyes, only to realise that the tent was in total darkness. Something had disturbed me, but my thoughts were groggy. Maybe I'd had a bad dream, or it was just my imagination due to the earlier encounter with the hyena.

Owen was sleeping soundly beside me, with just a murmur between deep breaths as he lay wrapped in his sleeping bag. I contemplated lying down again or searching in the dark for his torch. Instead, I listened and waited. Seconds later, I heard soft grunts, followed by a deep growl. There were lions in the camp!

In response, my heart missed a beat and started to race. The next grunt was louder, followed by a spine tingling roar from a passing lion. There was more than one, and they seemed to be dangerously close. Maybe they could smell the hyena from earlier or were intrigued by the dying light from the discarded torch. My body froze, as I fought the urge to shake Owen awake. Was it my imagination or could I hear every footfall? Was it a gentle breeze that shook the side of our tent, or the brush of a lion's tail?

For a moment, I contemplated calling for the guard, but dismissed the notion just as quickly. He was probably fast asleep, and I had no idea how the lions would react if I started yelling into the night. It felt like an eternity as I held my breath, not daring to make a sound or move a muscle. In my head, I counted to ten and listened again. I heard another growl, but the noise was faint. They were on the move. Within minutes, the campsite returned to silence. Sleep, when it came again, was listless. By the time Owen woke me in the morning, I was bathed in sweat.

We ventured out of camp just before dawn, and from the safety of the truck, watched the horizon burst into life as the sun made its appearance. By first light we were rewarded with the sight of thousands of wildebeest scattered across the savannah, grazing on green shoots from recent rains. Later, we spotted a handful of elephants, far in the distance. Most passengers took photos from afar, but there was no need, as the elephants were approaching with every giant stride. Ears flapping and trunks high, they slowed by our truck, and then turned towards a patch of woodland. Just as quickly, they disappeared, leaving behind footprints, a taste of dust and large dollops of dung.

Soon after, two lionesses were sighted, sitting together under an acacia tree, watching a lone gazelle, far in the distance. By now, the sun was biting and the early morning excitement began to fade. The lionesses slipped away, prompting calls from Michael that it was time for breakfast.

While back at camp, John and Beryl searched for lion prints and tried tracing their movements past our tents during the night. Others joined in for a while, each of us pointing out indents in the soft earth and looking for clues. John asked the guard if he'd heard the appeals for help, but he laughed away the question and went in search of more coffee.

Maybe it was the late-night antics, or just the fact that the weeks leading up to the trip had been demanding, but I remained as silent as our guard during breakfast. I felt my body shiver, despite the rising temperature.

I needed to go to the toilet but shied away from the stench and flies of the long-drop. Instead, I grabbed a hand shovel and loo paper, then made my way to the edge of camp. While hastily digging a narrow trench, I looked around to check if the scene was clear. Apart from the flies, it all seemed quiet. I dropped my shorts and underwear, and then squatted above the hollow that I'd scratched into the earth.

Moments later, I was joined by a troop of baboons. They appeared without warning and kept their distance while foraging in the undergrowth. Suddenly, an inquisitive youngster peeled away and bounded nearer. Another skirted behind my back and began to edge closer. I didn't know whether to shout out for help or remain silent, but knew it was time to finish what I'd earlier started. Two adult baboons sat in the shade of a nearby tree, grooming each other without glancing my way. One let out a yawn, revealing a set of sharp fangs. He then looked towards me and sat up straight, suddenly interested in what I was doing.

It was the guard that saved the day, running into the clearing, his arms waving as he shouted for the baboons to scarper. They bounded away to a safe distance, stopping by a tree to weigh up the scene. I hastily finished my business and reached for a water bottle, to wash my hands. As we returned to the tented area, I thanked the guard. He shrugged and managed a smile. 'You might be too skinny for the lions of the Serengeti, but never trust a baboon. I think you need to use the long-drop toilet next time, like everyone else. It might be smelly, but at least you won't have to worry about a baboon taking a chunk from your white bottom.'

We lazed away the remainder of the day under the shade of acacia trees. I tried sleeping in the tent for a while, but a bout of coughing left me edgy and lethargic for the sunset game drive. As soon as we returned, I ignored the offer of fireside drinks and opted for an early night.

The following day my condition slowly deteriorated. Not by much, but just enough to leave me feeling weakened, with a blocked nose and persistent cough. In any normal situation, the common cold is barely worth a mention, but in a few days I'd be venturing onto the lower slopes of Kilimanjaro, hoping to climb to the icy summit.

Thankfully, the itinerary included a stopover in a fenced encampment just outside one of the national parks. Surrounded by miles of open scrubland, it resembled a modern-day oasis, complete with a pool, cafe and outside bar. Unlike our time at the bush camp, we weren't alone, with two overland trucks parked outside the gates. The passengers from the parked trucks were already settled in. Some were in the pool, others lazed on loungers and a lively crowd propped up the bar, all with stories to tell about their time in Africa.

While we set up our tents, Michael explained that many of the adventure travel companies followed similar routes across Africa. This meant that passengers and crew heading in one direction, would occasionally encounter other trucks, coming from the opposite direction. For those in charge of overland excursions, these meeting spots are perfect for catching up on gossip and news.

Despite the appeal of evening drinks by the pool, I opted for an early night, but woke bleary eyed, with a croaky voice and tickly cough. After a simple breakfast, we faced one final decision. We could stay in the encampment and enjoy the amenities or travel to Arusha for the chance to wander the markets. Michael would drop the group in the town centre before heading towards the nearby airport to pick up two additional passengers. They'd both travelled from England for the chance to climb Kilimanjaro, and I knew them well.

One was my oldest brother, Dave. The other was his friend, Paul. I'd initially planned to travel to Arusha, to search for a worthy memento in the bustling market and enjoy a beer with Dave and Paul on their arrival. But all I craved now was rest and the chance to recuperate. The Kilimanjaro climb was only 24 hours away and to begin the trek with a head cold wasn't something I relished.

Before leaving for Arusha, Michael instructed us to pack away most of the tents. We left two standing, for those who'd chosen to remain at the camp. All our rucksacks were staying behind too, so that he could clean out the truck compartments while in Arusha. They were piled together alongside the two tents.

Most passengers opted to travel into Arusha, including Owen, and as they clambered on board, Michael called a meeting to explain the simple rules for those staying put. I'd be there with Beryl and two blonde girls from London, who'd rarely spent time apart since arriving in Nairobi. Even as Michael spoke, I could see their thoughts were elsewhere, their eyes drawn towards the camp entrance, where the pool and café waited.

The sun was already high and the flies made each of us fidgety as he gave a last brief. 'Okay, guys, we're going to be gone for about five hours, which means you can expect the truck to roll into camp at four this afternoon. It's a two-hour drive from here to the hotel at Marangu. I need you to be ready, as I want to be there by sunset. Alistair, you rest up and take those tablets I gave you. I'll let your brother know why you've stayed behind. The golden rule is never to leave any of these rucksacks or tents unattended. Not even for a minute. There is some valuable stuff here and you never know who is watching. I'll leave it up to the four of you to work out a system. There's plenty of shade in the tents, plus lots of water and although the café is expensive, it sells decent food.'

And with that, they were gone and I was standing alongside Beryl and the two skittish teenagers, who were wiping sunscreen onto their faces and whispering to each other. I wasn't in the mood for somersaults into the pool and the thought of food turned my stomach, so it made sense that I was the first to stay behind. I didn't want to be forgotten and asked them to consider taking over in a while. In response, Beryl made a show of wrapping her arms around the girls. 'Don't worry, Ali, we'll check on you every hour, for sure.'

The girls departed without a word or a backward glance, laden down with towels, books, portable music and sunscreen. Beryl traipsed a yard or two behind, turning to wave at me as she stepped through the open gate.

Our tents had been erected on a wide strip of lawn, close to the encampment fence. The rucksacks were located alongside, each filled with the necessary clothes and accessories for an overland trip and mountain climb. Initially, I used them as an ideal resting spot, with my legs stretched out on the grass and my back snuggled against their cushioned sides. Boredom led me to play with the short sword that I'd purchased from the tribesman. I found a pile of sticks and began chopping at them. This led to another bout of coughing, so I returned it to my daypack and lay back on the grass.

The grass strip was about 30 metres wide and stopped sharply at the tree line. Once or twice, I thought I saw monkeys high in the canopy, but instead of searching for wildlife I scrambled in my pack for headache tablets. Eventually, the tropical sun forced me into the nearest tent.

Beryl appeared with perfect timing and offered to take over, but I felt too lethargic to move. She returned soon after with a cool drink, which I happily accepted before sending her away once more. Hours later, I was holding my stomach, willing her to appear as the rumblings increased. Unable to wait any longer I ran through the open gate, into the pool area, where Beryl lay in the sun, a magazine covering her face.

The girls were relaxing in the pool, chatting with a group of tanned lads. While running towards the toilet, I shouted out to them. 'Your rucksacks are in that field and there's no-one looking after them.'

By the time I returned to the tents, Beryl was standing guard and quickly apologised for falling asleep. While I worked alongside her to pack away the tents, the truck made a noisy entrance into the compound, its horn beeping to gain attention. The girls arrived on the scene with perfect timing, just as the truck came to a stop.

I spotted my brother at once, his smiling face peering at me from the passenger side of the driver's cab. Michael was the first to disembark, but didn't seem to be in the mood for chitchat. His main aim was to ensure we completed a swift turnaround. He called for help to ensure the remaining tents and rucksacks were stowed in the designated compartments. While the equipment was being fed along a daisy chain of helpers, I waited for Dave and Paul to disembark. They stepped onto the grass, then ventured nearer to shake my hand. It was Dave that spoke first. 'I've heard you're not too well. Will you be okay for the mountain climb?'

I tried to make light of the pounding in my head and the pains in my stomach and initially dismissed his worries. With brotherly concern, he persevered and asked if I'd seen a doctor. I smiled and said, 'Dave, there are no doctors out here, but I'm sure I'll be fine. Besides, I need to be with you on the mountain, to make sure you don't go the wrong way.'

Paul let out a chuckle at my weak jest. He knew all about our family rivalry and had been a close friend to us both for many years. Although it was Sunday football that had brought us all together, playing for a pub team for many seasons, we were now seeking other pastimes. A few years earlier, they'd both discovered the joys of long-distance walks, including the Pennine Way, a 268-mile trek across the backbone of England that finishes just inside the Scottish border.

On one occasion, they'd even convinced me to give up a summer holiday to Tenerife with friends, in exchange for a 73-mile trek across the Lake District. This mountainous area of northwest England is renowned for its wide-open spaces, dotted with picturesque villages, bustling market towns and rolling farmland. It is here that you will find England's highest peak and deepest lake. The misty fells and secret backwaters have helped to inspire painters and poets and for those seeking solitude, there are a myriad of walking trails, from low-lying woodland to steep mountain passes.

Instead of bathers, T-shirts and party clothes, I needed to pack waterproofs and thick layers. Instead of a beachside hotel overlooking the Atlantic Ocean, I slept in a two-man tent each night, trying to ignore the bleats of nearby sheep. Along the way, Dave taught me to navigate across the hills and dales, using a map and compass.

Paul also taught me a few things as we traversed the countryside. He'd point towards fields of barley and explain the timely process of brewing crafted ales from natural ingredients. Each evening, after a long day's walk, we'd find a village pub to enjoy a hearty meal, washed down with locally brewed ale. By the end of the week, he'd weaned me away from mass produced, fizzy lager. Despite missing out on the bright lights and balmy nights of a Tenerife beach holiday, I'd enjoyed every mile of our trek across the hills.

Now they were in Africa, fit and ready to add Kilimanjaro to their growing list of completed adventures. Dave was keen to share how the trip from England had gone so far, but I couldn't concentrate due to the constant movement of people and luggage around us. The next voice I heard belonged to Chris, calling out to gain attention. 'Has anyone seen my rucksack? It's a brand new Berghaus and has my name tag on one of the straps!'

As Dave spoke, I spun around to search for Chris. He was in the rear hold, rummaging amongst the stash of luggage while asking for help from those nearby. Despite his growing anxiety, most passengers were too excited to listen and had already clambered on board. Within two hours, the truck would be at Marangu, one of the villages close to the base of Kilimanjaro. Finally, he raised his voice and this time everyone stopped to listen as the words boomed out. 'Alistair, did you watch over our gear all afternoon? My rucksack is nowhere to be seen!'

I felt the blood drain from my legs as the campsite fell silent. At that moment, all eyes were on me. I took a breath and said, 'Well yes, of course, but there was a time when I needed the toilet and...'

He was close to me now, his voice tense as he raised a finger. 'Didn't you have a system in place? Where were the girls when you decided to take a break?'

Beryl tried explaining, but Michael asked her to hush and called out for Peter, our driver. What we didn't know until then was that Peter used to be a tracker in the Tanzanian army. Throughout our time on safari, he'd seemed a quiet man, with a good sense of humour and a hearty chuckle. But he wasn't smiling now, as he studied the terrain. Then, without a word, he set off across the grass towards the trees. I gave chase, along with Michael, Chris, and Dave. With each wide stride I could hear Peter muttering to himself, and as we stepped into the woods he paused, then squatted on the ground.

He looked up and said, 'There were two of them watching you, bwana. See here and here–this is where they lay–maybe for many hours–just waiting for a chance. How long did you leave the luggage unattended for?'

I couldn't see what he was pointing at. To me, it was just mud, grass, and tree roots. I placed my hand on the ground, feeling for an indent, and stared up at Peter. 'I needed to go to the toilet and was only gone five minutes.'

'No matter, it is done. When did this happen?'

'Not long before you arrived. Maybe 20 minutes ago.'

He didn't seem to be listening and was already moving further into the woods. He walked for another few minutes, watching the ground the whole time, before stopping once more. 'This is where they dropped the booty and opened it up to see what they'd stolen. There might have been two bags, I can't be sure. But they will be long gone by now, and although I doubt it, they could be carrying a machete. I don't think we should give chase.'

Chris was the next to speak, his shrilled voice impossible to miss. 'But my gear for trekking up the mountain is in that rucksack. My camera is in there too and all the gifts I bought in Kenya.' He put his hands to his head, rubbed them across the tight curls and said, 'Oh man, this sucks. This seriously sucks.'

An hour later we were driving towards Kilimanjaro, and as the sun dropped towards a distant ridgeline, I sat in a corner seat, avoiding eye contact with Chris. My head pounded, not only from the head cold, but the feeling of despair that I'd let everyone down. The two girls had somehow avoided any finger pointing, and Beryl was deeply apologetic that she'd taken a nap.

The wind constantly rattled through the open sides and I felt a shiver run down my spine. Dave was nearby and I asked him to pass my rucksack over, so that I could locate a warm jacket.

'No problem,' he said. 'Where is it?'

'I'm not sure. In all the commotion back at camp, I didn't see where it got stored, but it should be in the partition next to you.'

His voice softened, tinged with concern. 'Ali, have you seen your rucksack since we boarded?'

'No, I've just been thinking about—'

'What does it look like?'

'You know, it's the blue and red one that I bought a few weeks—'

His deep voice cut above the din of the engine, asking out if anyone had seen a large, blue and red rucksack. In the last of the light, I could make out the outline of the passengers, each checking under seats and in the designated compartments. Even before the replies came back, I sensed it had also been taken.

Pretty in Pink

"Be brave. Take risks. Nothing can substitute experience."
Paulo Coelho

'We have a lost property section which you are free to scavenge, but I'm afraid it's sparse at the moment. I'm just about to give a presentation to the climbers and will assist you afterwards.'

I was talking with Erika, an elderly lady who still played a part in running the Marangu Hotel, a colonial style homestead that has been organising Kilimanjaro expeditions since 1932. After our brief conversation, she made her way to the front of the room, before calling for silence.

There were about 30 of us inside, all bristling with a mixture of anticipation and excitement. Some stood near the back, enjoying ice-cold beers, while most sat in comfy chairs, with their legs stretched out. Ceiling fans whirred overhead, trying to cut through the humidity, as Erika cleared her throat and began to talk.

'Good evening, everyone,' she began, 'and welcome to the Marangu Hotel. It has been a part of my life for many years and I hope you enjoy the overnight stay. I've climbed Kilimanjaro a few times and over the years have learned one or two of its secrets. This hotel and all the staff have helped thousands of people, just like you, to fulfil their dreams. I'd like to share some tips that might help you reach the roof of Africa.'

The room fell silent as she gave a brief history lesson, telling us about Johannes Rebmann, the German missionary who, in 1848, reported seeing a snow-capped peak just three degrees south of the equator. At the time, the London Royal Geographic Society didn't believe the findings and dismissed the notion that ice could be located so close to the equator, as a malaria-induced hallucination!

The Germans were the first again, this time with a successful summit attempt in October 1889, led by a German geology professor called Hans Meyer. He'd teamed up with an Austrian mountaineer named Ludwig Purtscheller and together with a local guide, they battled their way to the top. It had been Meyer's third attempt in as many years, with previous expeditions thwarted by heavy snow, thick ice and a lack of equipment.

Although we wouldn't be following in their exact footsteps, we'd get the chance to experience a journey through five ecological climate zones, starting with the cultivated land surrounding the base of the mountain. We soon discovered that the route takes climbers through tropical forest, where local hunters used to dig pits in the hope of snaring forest dwelling elephants. Further up, the trees dwindle, replaced by moorland, before turning into alpine desert and open scree, which leads to the snow-capped summit.

As Erika stopped briefly to take a sip of water, I overheard whispers from a nearby group about the frozen corpse of a leopard, found near the summit decades earlier. I smiled, remembering the opening lines of Hemingway's *The Snows of Kilimanjaro*, where he describes such an incident. The highest freestanding mountain in the world was indeed a place of wonder, and hearing Erika's stories made me realise it would be easy to get confused between fact and fiction.

Although my guidebook was filled with many facts and figures, it felt so much better to hear the information firsthand from someone who had grown up in the surrounding area. Erika had met hundreds of fresh-faced tourists over the years, all of them eager to climb the mountain. Some returned to the hotel after their climb, to recuperate or relax, and each had a story to tell about their time on Kilimanjaro.

For those attempting the climb, Kilimanjaro is often their first-ever high-altitude experience. Its lure is universal for many reasons, but being the highest mountain in Africa certainly helps. Since Hans Meyer's successful attempt, thousands more have tried, but not always in his footsteps. Throughout the years, alternative routes have been added, some more technical and isolated than others, allowing extra time on the slopes for acclimatisation. The hardest route is through the Western Breach, which involves a high-altitude scramble on exposed crags, covered in ice and snow. This route is for serious climbers only and requires the use of ropes, ice axes and crampons.

The route we'd chosen was the Marangu trail, which meant we'd stay in wooden huts during our time on the mountain. The simple lodgings are popular with those on a budget, but the direct route is not without its critics who say that trekkers are encouraged to ascend too quickly, and therefore risk falling ill, with mountain sickness. In response, it is now possible to add another day to this route, to assist with acclimatisation.

All those who venture onto the slopes need to be mindful of Acute Mountain Sickness, which occurs if climbers ascend too quickly. With less oxygen at higher altitudes and reduced air pressure, the symptoms include nausea, headaches and a shortness of breath, even when resting.

The worst-case scenario is if fluid accumulates in your lungs, leading to a serious condition known as pulmonary edema, which can lead to a coma or, at worst, death. Symptoms include an unsteady gait, increased vomiting and a gradual loss of consciousness. Experienced mountain guides continually check on their clients, but at high altitude, conditions can change rapidly. For all types of altitude sickness, the safest option is to rapidly descend! There are no official statistics on Kilimanjaro deaths, but estimates range from five to ten trekkers per year, plus of course there are fatalities among the support crew from time to time.

During our briefing at the hotel, Erika discussed the topic of altitude sickness at length. She also put any notion of relaxation out of my mind. 'Although you are sleeping in cabins, this is not a summer holiday. They are basic and the higher you climb the more rudimentary they become. Some of the lower huts sell beer, but in my opinion, drinking alcohol will hinder your efforts. My advice is to drink water until you return safely. Then you can enjoy a celebratory drink.'

Then she changed tack and asked, 'Who amongst you is aged between 40 and 60?'

A few trekkers put up their hands, including John, our Vietnam veteran. I could see him in the front row, scratching the newly formed beard he'd grown fond of during his time in Africa. Erika smiled at those with their hands held high. 'You will all do well, I am sure. You are still young enough to climb, but without the youthful vigour that might tempt you to walk too fast each day. The Swahili phrase that all of you in this room need to learn is *poli-poli*. It means slowly-slowly, and the tactic of walking steadily at your own pace will help get you to the top.'

She then asked for a show of hands, for those that were under 30. In response, a multitude of guests thrust their arms high. Erika gave a quick count and said, 'It seems that most of you are relatively young. Although you all look fit, it's quite possible that one or two of you might not make it to the top.'

As the crowd murmured, Erika explained her reasoning. 'For those that are young and fit, you might think the trek is relatively easy, especially during the first few days. The distance between the huts is comparatively small, but it's the gain in altitude that will affect you all. You must let your body adjust, as slowly as possible.'

After a sip of water, she continued. 'If you didn't take in any of the history of Marangu and the connection with past climbers, then please heed this one last piece of advice. Avoid the alcohol on sale in the lower huts, drink plenty of water, purchase a walking pole if you don't have your own and take your time each day to get to the next hut. I would like to hear that you all made it to the summit of Kilimanjaro. It is called Uhuru, which means freedom, and when you stand on the roof of Africa, there is no better feeling.'

There was a moment of silence as each trekker pondered her words. To close out the speech, she pointed towards me. 'Now, does anyone have any questions as I need to assist some climbers who are without the correct clothes or equipment? If anyone has any spare items they can donate, please see me afterwards.'

A middle-aged couple occupying two of the front row seats quickly stood up, their guidebook at the ready as they called her name. While she answered their questions, I went in search of Chris and together we entered a small room near the back of the hotel, where lost property was stored.

As warned, the choice was limited, with bags of odd socks taking up most of the cupboard space, along with an assortment of gloves, hats, a few jumpers that had seen better days and a pair of waterproof leggings, in mint condition. I offered Chris the first refusal, which he accepted with a gruff smile before making a smart move towards the leggings, followed up by a search for gloves and a determined attempt to find a jumper to fit his wide shoulders.

After loading up on suitable garments, he wished me good luck with the remaining items and went in search of his friend. Like me, he'd been wearing his walking boots when the thieves struck. That was one major consolation for us both.

Peter had kindly donated his rain jacket to me and I couldn't refuse the friendly gesture, even though the red waterproof, with ample zips and pockets, hung low to my knees! Regarding other clothes, my options were limited, and after searching through every cupboard

I returned to the hotel bar, dressed in a baggy woollen jumper and pink tracksuit pants!

To complement the look, I'd scavenged a pair of walking socks, one pale blue and the other, a dark shade of forest green. I'd been wearing walking shorts when the robbers struck, so that was another consolation. I still had sunglasses and a balaclava, which had been stowed in my daypack and therefore untouched by the thieves.

The hotel bar was buzzing with anticipation, as the excited patrons enjoyed a last drink or two before an early night. Dave came over to compliment me on the colourful outfit and handed me an ice-cold bottle of beer. We clinked glasses and I took a tentative sip. I went to take another, but thought back to Erika's words about alcohol and the mountain. Despite the medication that I'd taken, my head still pounded and I was constantly blowing my nose. I placed the bottle on the table and turned my attention to the images and paintings, displayed on the mottled walls.

I was surrounded by the history of Kilimanjaro, with black and white photos of climbers, standing close to a shimmering glacier. Many of the guides and porters that helped Hans Meyer during his expeditions would have been born and raised in the villages surrounding the mountain.

One of the most respected guides was Yohani Kinyala Lauwo, who was born in Marangu and spent his entire life in the area. It is said that he guided for 70 years, and at the time of his death, it was estimated that he might have reached 124 years of age! Without accurate records, no one can be sure, but there is no doubt he had an eventful life. As a mark of respect for his many years as a favoured guide, he was honoured upon his retirement by the Kilimanjaro Mountain Club.

The tradition of using local guides continues to this day, and we were pleased to find out that our support team lived close by. Just before the evening ended, Erika gave us one more piece of advice. 'Please take heed of your head guide and remember to treat the porters and cooks with respect. They work very hard to give you the best experience possible. Without them, your dreams cannot become reality.'

After a round of applause from the grateful audience, Erika was called upon to share more of her stories. I wanted to stay and listen, but another bout of coughing sent me heading to the doorway, in search of my bed.

Welcome to the Jungle

"It does not matter how slowly you go as long as you do not stop."
Confucius

After a leisurely breakfast, we prepared for our departure by loading up the minivan. While outside, I stopped on the lawn and gazed at the snows of Kilimanjaro, shimmering high above the earth. This time I wasn't looking at a music album cover, but the real thing. The summit looked far away and higher than I'd ever imagined, with speckled clouds creeping up the steep sides of the mountain. Dave joined me on the grass, smiling as he said, 'In three or four days, we'll be standing on the very top.'

'Let's hope so,' I said, not feeling half as confident.

'I hope we both make it, Ali, especially as it will be Mum's birthday when we head for the summit.'

In response to my puzzled look, Dave wrapped his arms around my shoulders. 'Did you forget about her birthday?'

With a sense of guilt, I smiled at her memory and said, 'Yes, Dave, I somehow forgot, but am glad you remembered.'

Since her death, I'd struggled with many things and remembering important dates was one of them. As for booking a trip that would take us to the summit on the same day as her birthday, that was nothing but pure luck. If it was an omen, I didn't feel a connection or a sense of higher purpose. I just felt like a man with a sore throat and pounding headache, about to embark on the trip of a lifetime. Although I didn't feel prepared, or confident of reaching the top, this didn't upset me. I'd take one step at a time and give it my best shot. It was all I could hope for.

After chatting with Dave, I decided to explore the grounds. Overnight, I'd discovered that the main residence, a whitewashed, colonial style building, was once a farmhouse. We'd camped in the grounds, which had been ample for our needs, but during the stroll I discovered a selection of holiday bungalows, set back behind the trees. Further on, I found a welcoming swimming pool set in a grassy area, protected by wide-leafed trees.

Birds continually came into view, each species more colourful and songful than the last. While walking back to the hotel entrance, I spotted lounge chairs and tables positioned close to the base of a tree, with commanding views of Kilimanjaro. If ever there was a place to relax and recuperate, I'd found it. I'd liked to have stayed for longer, to get to know the friendly staff and to enjoy walks into the local village. But even now, while surrounded by nature, the silence was being broken, with calls from Owen that the minivan was about to leave.

Throughout the drive to the park entrance, all eyes were peeled for the mountaintop, but gathering clouds hampered our search. Instead, I concentrated on the people that we passed along the road. Women dressed in bright colours sat on the verge, alongside bundles of freshly cropped bananas. Unlike the ones in my local grocers at home, these were shorter and stubbier, with dark green skins. One lady sold pineapples, and many others had oranges for sale, balanced three-high, into eye-catching pyramids.

With more time, I'd have liked to wander along the street, to shop for trinkets and chat with the locals. But our itinerary didn't include stopovers at this point and with reluctance, I watched the market stalls fade from view, as we continued our journey.

We drove towards a large set of wooden gates, which were opened briskly by a grinning attendant, dressed in green fatigues. Three men squatted on a mound of grass close to the entrance and watched as we passed by. Others stood nearer to the gates, stepping back to allow us through. I waved to the nearest, but received nothing in reply. It was Owen who brought me to my senses. 'I reckon they won't be smiling until they get picked as porters or cooks.'

Owen's words struck home as I studied the men outside the compound, each of them hoping to be called upon for work. Maybe there was a preferred set of workers, used over and over on a rotation system. There would have to be time off for recovery, especially for the porters, who were expected to carry heavy loads up the mountain to cater for the guests.

Inside the gates, we were met by smiling officials and ushered towards a wide desk to register for the climb. Other trekkers milled around, chatting casually and adding to the jovial atmosphere, while we confirmed our names and signed the registration book. I was then handed an official-looking document and instructed to read it at my leisure before climbing the mountain. While seated at a nearby bench, I studied the piece of paper. I'd been given an official permit to climb Kilimanjaro, which included an additional piece of information, stamped in the corner.

Bicycles, motorcycles, skiing, parachuting, gliding and all forms of flying are not allowed on any part of Kilimanjaro.

The words reminded me of a book that I'd once read, called *Bicycles up Kilimanjaro*. It's about two cousins, Nicholas and Richard Crane, who'd ridden (and carried) their bikes to the summit, in 1985. Nicholas is now a successful writer and broadcaster, but at the time of his Kilimanjaro attempt, he was a young man with a thirst for adventure and the audacity to try something new. While undertaking adventurous or demanding challenges, there are some participants that look for different ways to stand out from the crowd. Marathons have been run backwards or in rhino suits, and one man has hitchhiked around Ireland with a fridge, in the hope of a wonderful tale to tell at the end. (As a side-note, the plan worked, and his book has been a major success).

Nobody in our group was attempting anything quirky or unusual, except that I was wearing pink tracksuit pants! Mostly, we resembled any other collection of excited novices: unsure of how many layers to wear, constantly rechecking our bags, and posing for photos with the forest as a backdrop.

A boy approached with a selection of wooden poles and asked if we wanted to buy any. Owen negotiated a fee if we purchased in bulk and within seconds the boy raced off with a broad smile, after pocketing a handful of dollars. Dave handed his camera to a stranger and chaperoned us together for a quick photo, each of us proudly holding a walking pole.

After carefully stowing the permit, I decided to explore the surroundings. I spotted Owen's rucksack along with the others, in a sprawling pile. There were other items too, including plastic containers and sacks of food. Nearby stood a group of locals, chatting away while pointing at the stash of equipment. One man broke away and headed towards the perimeter fence. He was short and wore a black baseball cap, which he took off to wave for attention. Two men were standing on the other side of the fence and reacted to the call by racing towards him. Moments later, a side gate was opened to allow them to join the other porters as hired hands.

The man with the baseball cap then took charge of proceedings, as the porters divided the equipment in readiness to begin the climb. Some used webbing or ropes to tie the baggage to their backs and others balanced heavy baskets on their heads. While they made final adjustments, I studied their footwear, thankful that they all wore boots or enclosed shoes.

Although their clothes looked a little ragged in places, they seemed to be in similar condition to those I'd raided from the lost property cupboard. In contrast, Beryl had finally taken off her new waterproof jacket and was stuffing the coat into one of the sacks, while informing her quizzical porter that it was made from lightweight material, so he had little to worry about!

With little fanfare, the porters set off along the trail without a backward glance. I watched as they entered the forest in single file, wondering when I'd next see their faces. As soon as they'd departed, the man in the baseball cap strolled towards us, smiling widely in a friendly greeting. 'Jambo. My name is Edward and I will be your guide. Welcome to Kilimanjaro. I hope you are all feeling fit and have listened to the advice so far.'

He had sharp blue eyes that didn't miss anything. 'I see that some of you have your own walking poles. If you don't have one yet, please hire one before you leave the park entrance. It is illegal to chop wood in the forest and they will help you during the long journey up and down.'

His request was met with a scurry of activity as a few trekkers hurried off in search of walking poles. While waiting, I strolled towards a nearby signpost, informing me that we were at 1,860 metres (6,000 feet). Further ahead, I spotted another sign, strategically placed alongside the path. It was titled: *Points to Remember*. It included a list of basic information, including advice on drinking five litres of water each day. The following words were etched into the wood:

If you have a sore throat, cold or breathing problems, do not go over 3,000 metres above sea level.

A quick calculation told me that this was somewhere between Mandara and Horombo huts, during day two of our climb. I popped another vitamin pill, tried blowing the mucus from my blocked nose, and walked back to our group, just in time to listen to the departure speech.

Edward gathered us close, his voice strong and clear. 'We are about to head to the first hut. I hope you know by now that this is not a race. Please enjoy your walk through the forest. If you listen carefully, you may hear the call of monkeys. If you are lucky, you might spot them as well. As you will have seen, the porters and cooks have far more to carry than you do, but they will be waiting for us at Mandara.'

He then pointed towards the trees. 'The path through the forest is easy to spot. We will gradually gain altitude all day. Sometimes it will be steep and you might have to scramble over the roots of trees. In other places, close to streams, the path gets wide and boggy. Take your time though, as there is no hurry. Does anyone remember the number one rule for climbing Kilimanjaro?'

Beryl knew the answer and called out, 'Poli-poli.'

Edward smiled and said, 'Very good. What is your name, madam?'

'Beryl.'

'Everyone here, please take notice of Beryl, as she has learned an essential tip for climbing the mountain. There are many others, including the need to drink plenty of water every day. Some of the lower huts sell snacks and water and there are streams along the way. If you fill up from these, please use purification tablets.'

There was another flurry of activity as some climbers checked their supplies of water. Dave and Paul looked on with the assured knowledge that they were totally prepared. Although they hadn't trekked at high altitudes, they'd honed their walking skills while undertaking multiple long-distance walks across Britain.

Paul is the shorter of the two, with a similar height to me, which is just short of the national average. Although short in stride, years of playing amateur football and spending summers in the hills had conditioned his body to hard physical exercise. My brother stood close to him, a few inches taller and itching to get moving. Both were dressed in T-shirts and shorts, with battle scarred boots.

Edward then called out, 'Okay, the talking is over. It's time to climb the mountain. From tomorrow, you will see two peaks in the distance. The craggy one is called Mawenzi and the one with a covering of snow is Kibo. It is the tallest volcanic cone on Kilimanjaro and is where we will be heading in the days ahead.'

Then he instructed us to join him, as he began walking into the forest. Moments earlier, the path had been filled with porters; weighed down with an assortment of bags, empty water containers, and food. We followed in their footsteps, our boots digging into the soft mud, each of us carrying a daypack containing a filled water bottle, a rain jacket, snacks and a camera.

I didn't know what to expect when we first stepped into the forest. If there were any elephants or other large animals nearby, they were screened from view by the abundance of trees on either side of the track. My guess is that most forest dwellers would have been scared away by the excited chatter of each trekker, as we absorbed the sights, sounds, and smells of the tropical jungle. The birds weren't afraid though and with each step along the trail they seemed to grow in number, as they flashed past, or sang to us from the canopy.

Our pace was initially quick, and the path was narrow, with a blanket of lush vegetation all around. I tried searching for the sky, but the trees were tall, with weeping branches covered in shiny green leaves. They formed a wide canopy, which blocked most of the sunlight. Shards of light streamed through every gap, forming dappled shadows across the track. We occasionally came across intersections, where trekkers had forged new tracks along drier ground. All these diversions eventually converged with the main trail and most seemed as muddy as the last.

In steeper places, exposed roots threatened to trip us up as we waded through mud and splashed across puddles. Beryl discarded another layer within the first hour, stopping by a tree to wipe sweat from her brow. Thirty minutes later, she was searching for a lightweight poncho in her daypack, as a sudden downpour sent us dashing for cover.

The rain quickly cleared, giving voice to the forest. We didn't see any monkeys but were rewarded with birdsong, followed by fleeting glimpses of their colourful plumage as they darted across the muddy scar that cut the forest in two. Most tree trunks were covered with vines, some as thick as hemp rope. I pulled on one and it held firm, as my legs swung in the air. Chris also had a go and managed a far braver, Tarzan-like, swing. It was good to see him smiling again.

As instructed by Erika and our guide (many times), we trekked up in poli-poli style, taking many hours to complete a journey that Beryl would have blitzed in half the time if she'd been in the Peak District. But this wasn't a gentle trek across the hills of England and the strain was showing on her face. From time to time, we'd hear voices behind us and would stop to let porters walk past. Overladen with sacks and baskets, they returned our greetings before continuing at a steady pace. Minutes later, they were gone from sight.

During a water stop, I took advantage of the free time and stepped away from the path, into the forest. Unlike the muddy trail, the floor was firm and covered in leaves. I used my pole to swish aside huge ferns, feeling the tickle of insects on my neck. I brushed them away and squatted by the forest floor to gather a fallen leaf, now turning with age.

Only then did I notice the army of ants trailing across the ground. There were thousands on the move, foraging for food. They moved quickly and I stepped out of their way, deeper into the forest. The trees within reach looked far taller than the ones I'd grown up climbing in England, with exposed roots that crept across the forest floor. I peered towards the canopy, hoping to spot a monkey, but apart from a stirring of the leaves, little else moved.

I heard my name being called from afar. It was Dave, his deep voice booming through the forest. I decided to jog back to the trail, but paid the price with a coughing fit as I reached the group. While kneeling by the path, I heard Beryl call out to me, her words sinking home as I fought for breath. 'Alistair, I think you should just keep to the track from now on. We have a long way to go, and you're fighting a cold.'

After heeding her advice, I settled into a rhythm for the rest of the day's trek. By late afternoon, we emerged into a clearing in the forest, having made it to the huts at Mandara.

Aim High

"Take a chance, you never know what might happen."
Unknown

With running water plumbed in from a nearby spring and solar panels to produce electricity, Mandara could have been self-sufficient, except for the high number of trekkers that it had to cater for each day. Providing food and shelter for the climbers was its primary role, and by the look of the cheery faces in the compound, things were working well.

The set up included a series of large, A-frame huts, positioned in the centre of a wide clearing. There was plenty of space for trekkers to socialise after their trek through the forest. Some relaxed outside, while talking, reading, or eating snacks. Others were seated in the sunshine, lost in thought, while taking notes. I spotted one man at the edge of the clearing, camera poised to capture photos of the flora and fauna. I even heard pop music blaring from one hut and watched two female trekkers dancing together, while posing for photos.

I didn't know what to expect in the way of dinner, but was happily surprised to be served chicken stew and rice, washed down with a choice of water or juice. We were seated in long rows, rather like a banquet at a wedding, though instead of suits, shirts or dresses, we wore T-shirts, and rather than talking about a bride and groom, the topic of discussion centred on Kilimanjaro.

'How much water did you drink today?'

'Is the spring water safe to drink?'

'How much do you think we should tip the porters?'

'I heard it got down to minus 20 at the summit last week.'
'Someone told me that Kibo hut was full up yesterday.'
'Didn't some trekkers have to sleep in the corridors?'

While we were deliberating the differences between rumour and fact, the food kept coming. There was also tea or coffee, to help wash down the biscuits and cakes. Nobody went hungry and there wasn't a single complaint. We were all seated together in a communal dining mess, along with travellers from across the world. Surprisingly, there was very little interaction between the trekking parties. I usually enjoy talking with fellow travellers, but I could feel my throat rasping as the evening wore on. Someone in the group mentioned beer and I could see that other trekkers were already drinking from bottles. I thought back to Erika's advice, made my excuses and went in search of my bed.

I woke to a bright day, with barely a cloud in the sky. There was an air of anticipation, as each trekker prepared their kit. I had fewer clothes to worry about, and so far, the pink tracksuit bottoms hadn't made much of an appearance, except to ward off the evening chill. With porters, cooks and guides on hand, there was little to do but enjoy the boiled eggs, grilled tomatoes and sliced bread. Even the sweet tea tasted good. With a full stomach and a good night's sleep, I'd gained a spring in my step as I made my way onto the track for our early morning briefing by Edward.

We were about to leave the tropical forest and enter a landscape that resembled low alpine heath. Before we set off, Edward gave us one last piece of advice. 'The next camp is only 12 kilometres away and you all look fully rested and raring to go. Please stop to appreciate the fauna, but do not pick any wildflowers.'

He momentarily cast his eyes towards the sky before checking his watch. 'At the moment, the weather is clear. This means you will get to see the peaks of Mawenzi and Kibo. If you think they are near enough to touch, then think again and drink more water. The hard work will begin soon enough.'

He then pointed at me. 'Alistair, I hear you were sneezing and coughing in the night. Stay close to me and stop often, my friend. A man with the flu should not be on the mountain. Hopefully, it is just a simple cold.'

And with that, he set off and we followed behind. According to the sign that I'd read at base camp, I'd need to consider turning back within the next few hours, but we all knew that wasn't going to happen. Besides, the sun was shining, Owen had a stash of jokes to share, and John was going to tell us a story about his time in Vietnam. We had all the time in the world, a single track we couldn't get lost on and enough snacks between us to feed a small army.

We soon came across a tall, cactus-like plant, which Edward explained was a giant lobelia. Throughout the morning we discovered many more, but just like London buses, there seemed to be places where they were plentiful and other locations where they were nowhere to be seen. Each one offered the chance to stop and take panoramic photos of the vibrant green leaves against the windswept heather. As promised, we continually found wildflowers, but in all honesty, it was the twin peaks of Mawenzi and Kibo that gained the most attention. We were now far above the clouds, with far-reaching views across the forest, towards the cultivated zone that stretches towards the plains of Tanzania.

I also spotted trekkers from other groups, dotted across the undulating landscape in a colourful daisy chain. We never seemed to catch them, even when they stopped for a rest. Each time we approached, they stood as one, then strode off with a clatter of walking poles and moved steadily away. There was also a trickle of foot traffic coming down the mountain, but if the trekkers had reached the summit, they didn't mention it. Their strides were long, and their reddened faces looked strained. Without a word, they trundled past, towards the base of the mountain.

I enjoyed the isolation of being in a relatively small group. We were all different, but each showed respect to the others. John would often stop or divert from the path to take photos of the plants and then race to catch us up. We'd then listen between ragged breaths as he shared the name and description of his latest find. Chris and Steve stayed close together but were happy to join in if there was a joke to share. Owen moved between groups, chatting easily on numerous topics. He spoke with Paul for a while, each of them striding purposely across the track while discussing other places in the world to go trekking. During his time alongside Dave, the conversation turned to skiing trips, new countries to visit and our chances of making it to the summit. The sun inched across the sky, while we walked and talked.

All too soon, the day's trek came to an end as Horombo came into view. I tried counting the huts while we strode purposely towards them, but thirst was foremost on my mind and I gave up without a fight. I'd read in my guidebook that they could accommodate 120 trekkers, which meant that our group might be sharing a room with others. The A-frame huts were smaller than the ones at Mandara, positioned on an outcrop and shrouded in mist. I spotted a few trekkers by one hut, but the large group that we'd continually tried to catch, was nowhere to be seen.

I also recognised a few porters from the park headquarters. At the time, they'd been dressed in shorts and singlets. Now, as they carried provisions into a nearby hut, most were wearing quilted jackets, long trousers and gumboots. Within minutes of our arrival, we followed their lead, as each of us went in search of our luggage to add extra layers.

After a simple meal of mashed potato and grilled meat, I ignored Dave's call for a high-altitude game of cards and went in search of my bed. Our bunkhouse had a selection of spare beds and two strangers had knocked on our door to claim some of them. The man on the top bunk was clean-shaven, with cropped hair, while his friend below had a wild mop of curls and a grizzly beard. I mumbled a goodnight, snuggled into my sleeping bag and turned towards the wall.

Close to the Edge

"Never, never, never give up."
Winston Churchill

The night was long, and our uninvited guests initially jabbered away in a foreign language, despite the polite appeals for them to hush. It was Owen's coughing that woke me, followed by the realisation that my feet were like bags of ice. I hastily donned a pair of walking socks and wrapped the sleeping bag tighter around my body. Just as a semblance of warmth returned, the bearded man stirred noisily and let out a series of grunts. I opened my eyes and stared into the dark, just as he began snoring.

Hours later, I woke to the sound of birdsong and stepped into a bright morning. Beryl was up and about, clasping a steaming mug of tea. 'Morning, Ali. Have you seen the view from here?' I followed her gaze, towards the top of the mountain, wishing I had a camera at hand. There was Kibo, suddenly nearer, its flattened summit coated in white. In the early light, the snows glistened. Suddenly, it was becoming real.

When we spotted Edward, his usual smiling face had been replaced by one of concern. He gathered us all round and explained his problem. 'Jambo, my friends. I hope the night was good for you. Please eat well this morning, as you are now just one day away from the hardest part of your journey.'

He then took out a piece of paper. 'This is a permit for getting all of you a bed at Kibo hut. There is only enough room for 60 people, but there has been a problem with the booking system and too many people have been turning up. Some of those arriving late have had to sleep in the corridors.'

John was the first to speak. 'Hey man, we've paid for the accommodation already. That's not right. What happens if we don't get a bed?'

Edward held his gaze and nodded. 'Yes, it is a problem, my friend, and one that I will try to fix when we reach the park headquarters. But for now, I need a volunteer to help me out. The first trekker to arrive with a permit will secure beds for their group.'

It was Dave that put his hand up first. 'I'm happy to head up there.'

Edward dropped his voice. 'I appreciate the gesture, but you need to be aware that overexertion at this stage might cost you a bid for the summit. You will not be alone though, as my head porter will go with you. If you accept the task, it will help to ensure we have beds for the night.'

He stopped talking for a moment, to let the words sink in, before continuing. 'You have to understand that your body might not adjust quickly enough, to the higher altitude.'

Dave smiled easily and said, 'Truthfully, I feel as right as rain. I've slept well, despite the coughing in our room. I'll breeze up there for sure, but will take it steady.'

Dave accepted the permit and stowed it away carefully. After a swift breakfast, he set off along the trail with the head porter, both waving and smiling for the camera. Shortly after, we followed suit, but at a slower pace.

The trek to Kibo hut can best be described as a long-distance pub crawl with friends. I remembered the beginning, enjoyed the middle, but the ending was hazy. It started well enough, with bright skies and warm sunshine, as each of us searched in the distance for Dave. Gradually, the jokes and banter dried up, as we settled into a steady pace. Until now, my breathing had felt normal, but as we slowly gained altitude, each new breath became harder to catch. The change was minuscule at first, but whenever we stopped for a water break or snack, it seemed harder to get moving again.

We'd entered a landscape known as the *Saddle*, a windblown semi-desert, which separates the peaks of Kibo and Mawenzi. Ironically, the lesser-climbed peak, Mawenzi, looked far more appealing, with its crags, gullies and ridges. Kibo looked tamer, even though it was higher and coated in snow.

Thousands of boots trampling over the same route, year after year, have produced a prominent scar across the Saddle. Volcanic rocks littered the landscape, but the pathway had been kicked clean and we trekked unheeded. The Mars-like surface of the plateau seemed to be devoid of any noticeable plant life, apart from lichen and moss, clinging to volcanic rocks.

Each hour seemed harder than the last. Not by much, but the incremental rise in altitude soon began to tighten its grip. For a while, Beryl went quiet and trudged near the back. After a lengthy stop for water and snacks, she found her voice again. My voice was croaky, but I'd paced myself all day and used the walking pole to assist my passage. Owen was the one who worried me. His usual banter had vanished, replaced by short, sharp replies.

It was Chris who first spotted the tin roof of Kibo hut, shimmering in the rarefied air. For a while we got excited and picked up the pace until we realised that it never seemed to get any nearer. We then lost it for a while, but finally the track turned and Kibo hut was in sight again. I could see its green roof, perched below the main trail that led to the peak of Kilimanjaro.

Beyond the hut, the ground seemed to rise sharply and from afar I could see the scar made from thousands of boot prints that had etched their mark in the scree. The path wasn't a straight line to the summit. Instead, it followed a zig-zag pattern, due to the steepness of the terrain. This is where we'd be in about ten hours, but first, I needed more water, a taste of warm food, and a bed.

By now, some of our group resembled a jaded army patrol, silently crossing the parched ground in single file. Paul and Chris didn't seem affected in the slightest and surged ahead. During the final approach to Kibo hut, a familiar figure appeared at the doorway. While I approached in short, laboured footsteps, Dave bounded down the track to greet us. I heard him speak, but couldn't decipher the exact words. He seemed to be telling our group about his trek and how he'd been the first to the hut. I heard his laughter and managed a smile as I made my way towards the entrance. While Dave continued to chat away, I sat on a nearby step, peeled off my daypack, and asked if he had any water.

If the shimmering peak of Kibo was visible, I didn't notice. I heard Edward congratulate Dave on claiming our beds, followed by more laughter. Then Beryl was shaking me awake, informing me that dinner was ready. We sat around a wooden table, in a small room with whitewashed walls. Dave's deep and cheerful voice carried far in the close confines, and I tried my best to focus. The food appeared quickly, but tasted cold and bland. After a humbled apology, we were soon rewarded with boiled eggs from the nearby kitchen, along with sliced bread and steaming bowls of mashed potato.

I played with the food and then made a brave decision to visit the long-drop toilet. The near freezing conditions helped, as well as a blocked nose, but the thought of returning to it again, soon turned my stomach. I noticed Owen by the side of the hut and went over to say hello. In the last of the light, the crags of Mawenzi peeked through a fine trail of lingering clouds, now tinged in pink. Pockets of snow lay in deep gullies, and the first of many stars began to shine through the gathering darkness.

Edward called us back to the hut to hear his final brief. 'I hope you have tried to eat. Although the food may not look appealing, it is important for your energy. Now you must prepare your kit, as I don't want anyone searching for headtorches or trying to fill up water bottles before we head off. After you have done this, try to get some rest and I will wake you at midnight.'

He paused before asking, 'Are there any questions?'

Beryl asked the one we'd all been thinking. 'How cold will it be at midnight?'

'When you wake, it will be around minus five, but it could get down to minus fifteen during the early hours. Remember to store water bottles away from the outside pockets of your daypacks, or they might freeze. Wrap up well, and if you have cameras, keep them covered–otherwise they will not work at the top.'

Then she asked, 'What if we feel sick on the way up and have to turn back?'

'It is my job to check on you all during the ascent. There will be others to assist, so if you need to turn back, we will help.'

I'd stayed under his radar until now and was hopeful of a hasty exit towards the dormitory. He noticed me stepping away and said, 'Alistair, you have done well to make it this far. Be careful from now on and be honest with me during the climb. I think it's time you got some rest.'

Before heading to bed, I put on the Macmillan T-shirt, followed quickly by my pink tracksuit pants and Aran jumper. Owen stashed his T-shirt in his bag, mumbling something about putting it on in the morning. Moments later, he was tucked up in a nearby bed, completely covered by his sleeping bag.

Sleep, if it came, was listless and fitful. Despite the thick jumper and sleeping bag, I could feel the cold seeping into my bones. In desperation, I called out to see if anyone had more layers for me. The only replies I got from those around me were hacking coughs and deep snores. Just after midnight, the overhead lightbulb came to life, followed by Edward's voice by the open doorway. 'It is time now. Please grab your things and make your way into the dining room for porridge and tea.'

Still yawning, I scrambled in the half-light for the rest of my clothes, thankful for the warmth as I zipped up the bright jacket borrowed from Peter. As the others stirred to life, I heard mumbles about the cold as they foraged in their packs for socks, gloves and hats.

It was Owen's turn to play with the food, and in silence we watched Dave and Paul devour theirs. Beryl and John whispered in the shadows and helped each other with their kit. Someone opened the door and we walked outside into the darkness. A crescent moon offered a glimmer of natural light but was soon obscured, as each trekker turned on their headtorches. For a while, we traipsed around the stone building, calling out names to ensure we were with the right group. Edward pulled us to our senses as he called for attention. 'Come here, all of you, and listen carefully.'

He gave us instructions as we huddled together in the darkness and whispered about the biting cold that stung our faces. Silently, we formed a ragged line and began walking up the steep pathway. Edward was true to his word and stayed close to me during the long, torturous night. In the darkness, we lost our footings, stumbled and cursed. More than once, I bent over and coughed until it hurt.

If this was what the holiday brochure meant about adventure travel, it was rapidly losing its appeal. A raw throat and a frozen water bottle are not good companions. It didn't matter, as I was too tired to contemplate the act of stopping, finding the water bottle, unscrewing the top and trying to match the rim with my mouth. Better to keep moving instead, though with every two steps up, the loose scree sent us down another.

Soon after, Edward called for a brief halt, to assist a climber with their bootlaces. During the unplanned stop, I began dozing off while leaning on my walking pole. The solitude didn't last for long, as Chris patted me on the shoulder, his croaky voice breaking the still of night. 'Wake up, Ali. It's time to go. I bet you wish you had your fancy climbing gear to wear, rather than a pink pair of pants.'

On another day, in a different location, I'd have chuckled at his words. Now that he mentioned it, my legs felt numb, but luckily, I still had the balaclava. With my face protected, I followed Chris and tried counting to ten, then a hundred, but all too soon the game was forgotten. It was all too hard. I heard noises and couldn't contemplate where they were coming from. They grew louder and then I saw the dark smudge of someone passing me by, followed by another. The procession was at least ten strong, all with glaring headtorches that fleetingly allowed me to study the weary expression on Beryl's pale face.

Someone asked how much further and there was no answer. Maybe it was minutes later or far longer, but they asked again, this time louder. Until then, I'd been unaware that Edward was behind me, his voice cutting through the night. 'Well done, my friends. We are now at Hans Meyer Cave. Let's stop for a break.'

My torchlight caught the shape of a man squatting alongside me, offering a tin mug, filled with tea. I couldn't find the strength to thank him as I held the drink in my gloved hands. The sensation of warm, sweet tea against my parched, trembling lips triggered a series of coughs. I finished the drink, placed the mug down, and lay on the cold, hard floor.

I had no idea how near we were to the summit, but didn't dare ask, in case the coughing started again. As for the cave itself, it was too dark to see what it looked like. Was it deep or just an overhang? We hadn't scrambled through an entrance, or had we? I closed my eyes and hoped the pain and cold would go away.

'Alistair, you must stand up. It is time to go. Give me your pack.'

Trancelike, I peeled off my daypack and handed it over without looking to see who was requesting it. I was too tired to care. Then we started to walk again, and I thought I heard Beryl call out my name.

Sometime later, my eyes began drooping as we trudged in single file up the steep track. Then the dreams started:

I was back in my childhood bedroom, holding an album cover with the image of Kilimanjaro, and my mum was calling me to come downstairs for dinner. I heard music and voices from the living room. It was Christmas, with a black and white movie on TV, showing James Stewart running along a snow-lined street. Mum was seated in her favourite armchair with a cup of tea. She looked up, with a look of concern on her face, and asked if I was okay.

I woke with a jolt, after tripping into the person in front. I mumbled an apology, but no one answered. After rubbing my eyes, I thought I could see a glimmer of light peeking above the darkened outline of the mountain. Then Edward spoke. 'Alistair, have you been sleepwalking? Please get to your feet as we are at Gilman's Point. You are very close to the roof of Africa.'

I tried to stand, but my head swam, causing me to remain on my knees. I'd heard him mention the roof of Africa, which meant we were somehow at the summit. But where were the flags? Just as the sun made an appearance, I spotted the crater, surprisingly close and sprinkled with snow. Like a boxer who'd been punched too hard, I tried clearing my head in readiness to continue the fight. Then suddenly, my stomach began to form knots, followed by painful spasms. I let out a deep moan and leaned towards the crater rim. The morning's porridge came out in a watery burst, burning my throat as it splattered against ice and rock.

Edward was talking to me, but I couldn't decipher his words. Someone gave me water and after a long gulp I opened my eyes. Owen was sitting close by, his eyes dilated. When Edward spoke, the words sounded soft and sincere. 'I am sorry, my friends, but this is the end of your adventure on Kilimanjaro. You must both descend quickly, along with Beryl. One of my guides will stay with you.'

'T-shirts,' I mumbled. 'We need a photo with the Macmillan T-shirts.'

Owen rummaged for his T-shirt and placed it across his body. I whipped off my jacket and jumper, somehow ignorant of the bitter cold as I proudly sat alongside him in my T-shirt. Paul noticed a wooden plaque declaring that we'd made it to Gilman's Point. It was sitting on a rock and he passed it over. We held it between us, trying to smile as Dave captured the moment, with the crater behind us and pockets of snow by our feet. Edward soon grew restless and called out that it was time to start moving. Just before they left, Dave put an arm around me and said, 'Mum would be proud.'

After a pause, he spoke again. 'Ali, do you remember about—'

My voice was barely a whisper. 'Her birthday. Yes, I remember. Please let me know what the view is like from the top.'

And with that, the coughing started again. I didn't have the strength to talk anymore and could feel my head swimming. I felt a tug on my arm and turned to face one of the guides. I didn't recognise him, but he was calling my name. In that moment, it felt as though he was miles away as his words drifted overhead. Owen stood close by, taking a last-minute photo of Beryl by the crater's edge. Then suddenly we were stepping off the ridge, and the ground fell away, as our boots bit into the loose scree. Despite the pounding in my head, I could hear the guide's voice, urging us downward, towards safety.

Our guide took giant steps and bounded down the loose rocks with ease. We tried following suit, but trembling legs and gasping lungs held us back. The tactic eventually worked, and within a few hours, we began to find our voices. By now, we'd bypassed Kibo hut and were heading to Horombo. By the time we arrived, I'd finally caught my breath. Only then did I have the strength to discover more about our mystery guide.

'My name is Oscar,' he said quietly.

'Did you hand out tea at the cave?'

'Yes, of course. I was at Kibo hut when we set off and stayed at the back throughout the night, to ensure nobody went astray. You looked poorly at Hans Meyer Cave, and I didn't think you would make it to the crater. That's why I carried your pack. I hope you feel proud that you made it that far.'

I suddenly felt humbled. This tall, unassuming man, with an awkward smile and a frizz of hair, had been part of the reason I'd made it to Gilman's Point. He'd also led us back down safely. Later that day, the successful summiteers arrived back at Hormobo hut, sharing tales about the biting cold and view from the top, while surrounded by the snows of Kilimanjaro.

A day later, weary but happy, we all arrived back at the park headquarters and stood patiently while Edward handed out completion certificates. There was an air of joviality, with many other trekking parties arriving on the scene. For nearly a week, we'd been considering the right amount for a tip, and Dave had constantly conferred with other walking groups. He handed over a bundle of cash from us all. Edward counted it quickly, shook Dave's hand and walked across to Oscar, who was standing alongside the porters and cooks. They formed a tight ring and quickly distributed the money, according to their own system. Afterwards, one or two broke away from the group and shook hands with the nearest trekkers.

Edward then called out that it was time to sing! He began to clap and asked for help from the porters. One man, dressed in gumboots, a knitted jumper and dark pants, took the lead. His voice was loud but tuneful and, with little effort, the surrounding porters soon joined in. Together, they performed the 'Kilimanjaro Song', which is sung to celebrate a successful climb.

Success comes in different forms and I understood why they looked so happy. They would soon be heading home, and no one had been injured or gotten too sick. Everyone was smiling, most had made it to the top or the crater rim, and the tips had evidently been enough.

They sang as only Africans can. The hairs on the back of my neck came alive as the clapping and singing filled the air. Partway through the song, I looked around, to study our group. Beryl's hair was as matted as her mud-splattered face, but she was smiling widely and hugging Owen. The two Californians were arm in arm with a tuneful porter. John looked rugged and proud, with a newly formed beard and weary smile, as he reached out to shake Paul's hand. While clapping along with the porters, I tried listening to every word. I recognised the places we'd seen and experienced but didn't know for sure what the song was about. Sometime later, I discovered the words and their English translation.

Kilimanjaro, Kilimanjaro, Kilimanjaro, mlima mrefu sana
(Kilimanjaro, long mountain journey)
Na Mawenzi, na Mawenzi (And Mawenzi, and Mawenzi)
Na Mawenzi, mlima mrefu sana (And Mawenzi, long mountain journey)
Ewe nyoka, ewe nyoka (As a snake, as a snake)
Ewe nyoka, mbona waninzungukaa (As a snake, it winds all around)
Jambo, jambo bwana (Hello, hello sir)
Habari garni (How are you?)
Mzuri sana (Very fine)
Wageni, mwakaribishwa (Foreigners, you're welcome)
Kilimanjaro, hakuna matata (Kilimanjaro, there is no problem)

Tembea poli-poli, hakuna matata (Walk slowly, slowly, no problem)

Utafika salama, hakuna matata (You'll get there safe, no problem)

Kunywa maji mengi, hakuna matata (Drink plenty of water, no problem)

Second Chance

"A second chance doesn't mean anything if you didn't learn from your first."

Anurag Prakash Ray

That should have been the end of the story. After all, Kilimanjaro isn't the kind of place that you usually get to return to twice in a lifetime, unless you're a mountain guide! Thanks to the efforts from Owen, we'd collectively raised over a thousand pounds for Macmillan, and our lives quickly returned to normal.

Weeks turned into months, and the years flew past. I began travelling further afield, but never for more than three weeks at a time. First it was Vietnam, then New Zealand, followed by a scuba diving holiday to the Red Sea (with Owen). I even borrowed Dave's bike on one occasion, to cycle 900 miles across Britain, along with two friends. This was also a charity challenge to raise money for Macmillan. Along the way, I nick-named his bike, *The Donegal Flyer*, in memory of our mum.

By now, I had an enjoyable career with General Motors, and as this took shape, so did other parts of my life. At a local gym, partway through a circuit training class, I bumped into a girl. A few years later, during a whirlwind day trip to Iceland, I asked Fran to marry me as we bathed in the turquoise waters of the Blue Lagoon. Two years later, we tied the knot.

Blonde, adventurous, caring and fun, she is often the life of the party. Although two years younger than me, she'd already travelled extensively, including a gap-year jaunt around the world. I still hadn't been away from the country for longer than three weeks.

This all changed one winter's day, when General Motors unexpectedly announced the closure of its car manufacturing facility, in my hometown of Luton. At the age of 38, I was to be made redundant. That evening, I spoke with Fran about the chance to travel far and wide, using the unexpected payout to help fund the trip. Luckily, she agreed and by the time we'd finished a bottle of wine, our wish-list of places to visit was complete.

After waving farewell to family and friends, we set off on our round-the-world adventure. Along the way, we worked as conservation volunteers in the jungles of Ecuador and signed up for Spanish school to learn the language. In the Andes of Peru, we hired donkeys and a guide to tackle a remote mountain pass. Later, we trekked along the Inca Trail, before heading overland to Bolivia to explore the high-altitude plateau. Near the edge of a mining village, we stumbled upon the remains of Butch Cassidy and the Sundance Kid, two of the most famous outlaws from the Wild West. Days later, we were deep underground in a silver mine, running for our lives from an explosion.

After returning to the UK for a week, we prepared for a trip to Africa, which would include an overland journey by truck. Now that General Motors had closed the car plant, it also seemed like a perfect time to try our luck for a new life in Australia. But first, there was a homemade movie I needed to watch.

Before heading back to Africa, I called upon Dave to watch the holiday video that he'd made, all those years before on Kilimanjaro. As the TV came to life, the memories came flooding back. Dave had captured the moment we all set off, with smiles for the camera and action shots of us swinging from vines in the forest. I enjoyed the footage of Owen striding across the Saddle, alongside John and Beryl, all of them waving to the camera as they passed by.

During the night-time trek to the summit, his camera had been safely stored away in his pack, to stop it from freezing up. The next time it came to life was to capture the moment they'd all reached the top of Kilimanjaro. The guide must have been holding the camera, as there was a close-up of Dave at the summit, along with Paul, John, and the two lads from California. Then the camera changed angle, to point towards the wooden sign that marked the peak. Although it was partly covered in stickers from previous climbers, the bold words in yellow were easy to read.

Congratulations, you are now at Uhuru Peak,
Tanzania, 5895 Metres, ASL.
Africa's highest point and the world's highest free-standing mountain.

When Hans Meyer stepped onto the summit on the morning of the 6th October 1889, the scene would have been very different. There wouldn't have been a sign at the top, or a queue of trekkers waiting for their turn to stand on the roof of Africa. It is said that he raised a German flag and named the top as Kaiser Wilhelm's Peak, in honour of the emperor of Germany.

To prepare for my second attempt, I also packed a flag, along with a selection of vitamin tablets. With luck, I'd make it to the top with Fran. Along the way, we'd walk *poli-poli* and drink plenty of water. Once again, Kilimanjaro was calling.

One Margarita

"No man ever steps in the same river twice, for it's not the same river and he's not the same man."
Heraclitus

The British Airways flight from London to Nairobi took off with perfect timing. As we rose into the winter sky, I peered out of the nearest window. Far below, I spotted a gridlocked motorway, filled with early morning commuters. Seconds later, the cars and trucks had vanished, replaced by mottled clouds. I kept my face to the window, hoping for the clouds to disperse. For a fleeting moment, a gap appeared, offering a faraway sight of green fields. Then, within a blink of an eye, there was nothing but whiteness below, as the plane burst into blue skies. As we levelled out, it suddenly struck me that I had no idea when I'd next see England, as we'd booked one-way tickets to Africa.

Sometime later, I worked out how to navigate through the list of movies and TV shows on offer. In truth, no amount of blockbusters or in-flight beers could quell the anxiety of leaving close family behind. Dad was not convinced we'd soon be meeting in Australia. His parting words were hard to swallow. 'Take care, son, but I might not visit–I'm getting too old to travel.'

Our plan was simple. We would travel from Kenya to Tanzania, for the chance to climb Kilimanjaro. From there, we'd head to the island of Zanzibar to relax on the beach, before flying to Zimbabwe to join an overland tour. The truck would weave a path through southern Africa, taking eight weeks until our arrival at Cape Town. From there, we'd make our own way to Johannesburg for the flight to Sydney, Australia.

After touching down in Nairobi, we spotted our names in the arrivals hall, being held high by our planned pickup. An hour later, while in the confines of the Silver Springs Hotel, Fran got chatting to a few tourists by the pool. We soon discovered that they were about to embark on an overland journey to Cape Town. They'd flown into Nairobi from various parts of the world and were now politely chatting together, exchanging names while checking out their crew-mates for the months ahead. There looked to be a few that were travelling solo, along with a mixed bag of couples and friends, all in search of an African adventure.

Fran mentioned we were on a similar trip and would start our overland journey from Zimbabwe. After comparing notes and dates with one of the passengers, she quickly realised that our paths would cross again in a few weeks, as we'd signed up with the same travel company. We wished them well, with plans to meet again in Zimbabwe.

Later, we attempted a stroll outside the hotel but were advised by a concerned security guard to stay inside, or to use one of the taxis parked on the roadside. Feeling peckish and in the mood to explore, we jumped into the nearest taxi and asked for a recommendation. The driver smiled and said, 'There is a restaurant called Carnivore, that is popular with tourists. I can take you there, no problem.'

Suddenly, I remembered back to my time in Nairobi with Owen, and after conferring with Fran, we set off on a trip down memory lane. Our driver chatted amicably as we drove out of the city centre, asking about our trip from England and the length of time we planned to stay. It didn't take long until he asked if we wanted to go on a safari, as he knew a guide that would take us. We declined the offer but agreed to use him again for the return journey.

The restaurant door was opened by a man in a white uniform, smiling as he ushered us inside. 'Good evening sir and madam. Welcome to Carnivore ...'

Just as before, I was handed an inch high flag and told to keep it flying for as long as I wanted. Fran also had a flag, which she placed in a designated holder on the table while studying the menu, which included charcoal roasted meats, crocodile and ostrich, plus the traditional favourites of lamb and beef.

Sometime later, while searching for the toilet, I discovered the outdoor area. The firepit was unlit and the place was in darkness. It had been a long time ago that I'd sat nearby with Owen, listening to fireside stories from fellow travellers. Although those days were now gone, the memories remained strong. Now, I was ready for more adventures and with a spring in my step, I returned to our table, where Fran sat, with her flag lowered.

After tipping the waiter, we headed back to the hotel in the same taxi. Once again, the driver asked if we were after a safari guide but wasn't too pushy when we declined. Instead, he turned on the car radio and twiddled with a dial until he found a music station. I recognised the song at once and asked him to turn up the volume. As we travelled through the darkened streets, I listened to the words and thought back to my time in Africa with Owen.

Jambo
Jambo Bwana
Habari Garni
Mzuri Sana

By early morning, we were on a modern shuttle bus heading to Tanzania. Any thoughts of admiring the views of the passing landscape quickly dissipated, as I fell into a deep sleep. Sometime later, we effortlessly passed through customs. By the time we arrived in the bustling town of Moshi, the sky was a fiery red. We were close to Kilimanjaro National Park, but the mountain was shielded from view by a haze of clouds. Instead of searching for a snowy peak, I turned my attention to the multivitamins and herbal tablets that I'd purchased at Heathrow Airport.

For my second attempt at Kilimanjaro, I tried involving Fran in the decision-making process, but her response was always the same. 'You're the expert on Kilimanjaro, not me. I'm sure you've discovered by now, the best and most enjoyable way to get to the top.'

I was no expert, but I'd learnt a few things from the earlier trek. This time it felt right to try our luck with tents, rather than wooden cabins. I was hoping the Machame route would be quieter. More importantly, it also added another day, to assist with acclimatisation. The decision was also made to have a night of luxury before the trek, in a family-run hotel, just outside town.

After a quick dip in the warm waters of the outdoor pool, it was time to enjoy a few drinks before dinner. A detailed mural of a charging elephant graced one wall of the thatched roof bar. We hopped onto two bar stools and were swiftly joined by a beaming barman, dressed in a dark blue blazer emblazoned with the hotel logo. 'Jambo! Would you like a gin and tonic, madam? And for you sir, how about an ice cold, Tusker beer?'

It felt good to be back in Africa! Along with the cold beer, I gulped down a selection of herbal tablets. While ordering another drink to mask the aftertaste, we were joined by the tour guide representative, to discuss the logistics of the climb.

She waltzed into the bar, adorned in loose flowing robes, gold bracelets, and high heels, calling to the barman for a margarita. We soon discovered that her dad owned the trekking company and because of sickness with a staff member she'd been sent on a last-minute errand to visit us at the hotel. Despite our enquiries, she tried steering the topic away from Kilimanjaro, to her recent business trip to London. With dreams of becoming a marketing manager, it soon became clear that the topic of mountain trekking was not high on her wish-list.

We didn't have many questions to ask, except for the pickup time in the morning, along with any news about the trekking conditions.

The responses we got were short and sharp. 'You'll be picked up at seven in the morning. Please do not keep the driver waiting. As for the trekking conditions, I'm sure they're fine. We haven't had rain for a while, so you won't need walking poles.'

Compared to the atmospheric and fun presentation given by Erika many years earlier, it felt like a letdown. By now, her cocktail was all but finished and she declined our offer of another one. Instead, she drained the glass and turned to face us. I thought she was going to wish us good luck for the climb. Instead, she said calmly, 'Please remember to bring your tent tomorrow.'

The throwaway comment caught us by surprise, and in response I asked her what she meant. She repeated the instruction again, this time a little louder and slower, in case we hadn't understood. 'You will need to bring your tent in the morning.'

Was this some type of joke? I sat up straight and looked her in the eye. 'You never told us that when we booked on the internet. I'm sure it said the trip was all-inclusive.'

She managed a thin smile and said, 'I'm not in charge of online bookings, so cannot comment. If you didn't bring a tent from England, you can hire one from me. The cost is 80 US dollars and I only take cash.'

She then looked at her watch and said, 'I have to go soon and need an answer. Would you like a hired tent or not?'

Fran's cheeks ripened as she replied to the rep. 'We don't want to hire anything, as we've already paid for the trip. I remember reading on the payment form that everything was included–even a tent!'

I followed up with another flurry. 'Look, this is obviously a ploy to get some money out of us at the last minute. Of course we need a tent, but I'm sure we could have purchased one back home for the same amount.'

She ignored our complaints and sat stony faced. 'As I said before, any issues with online bookings are not my problem. Would you prefer a two or three-man tent?'

Although angry, I was determined to enjoy the rest of the evening without her. With thoughts in place to raise the issue with her dad, I reached into my wallet. As I did so, she pushed back her stool and brushed a loose hair from her blouse. Just before extracting any cash, I said, 'I've only got 50 dollars and will need a receipt.'

Her reply sounded curt and far too confident. 'That's too bad, as I haven't got a receipt book.'

Instead of handing over the money, I managed a smile and said, 'Now that I think about it, I reckon we'll be okay without hiring a tent.'

Her eyes widened in surprise. 'But where will you sleep?'

By now, the barman was close by, silently drying glasses from behind the bar. I caught the concerned look on his face as I turned towards the young woman. 'Please understand that we chose your dad's company as he promised us a trip to remember, with no hidden extras. If there's no tent for us, we'll squash in with the guide. I hope he doesn't snore as much as I do. Now if you'll excuse me, we're off for something to eat.'

I expected her to call us back. But as we strolled past the grinning barman towards the restaurant, the only sound I heard was the clatter of high heels, heading to the car park.

The following morning, a driver arrived to take us to the starting location for the Kilimanjaro climb. His timing was impeccable. He found us in the breakfast room, first in line for the buffet. The smell of grilled bacon and fried eggs filled the air, but the driver was in no mood to wait around, insisting we move with a degree of urgency. 'Come, please. Your guide will be waiting, and I don't want to get into trouble.'

A waitress appeared with two bacon sandwiches wrapped neatly in a napkin and handed them over with an apologetic shrug. Maybe it was too early for conversation, but as we loaded our kit into his minivan, our driver didn't seem keen on small talk. The vehicle eased out of the hotel gates into a narrow lane shrouded by early morning mist, as we went in search of Machame Gate, where our trek would begin.

We were not the only ones awake. The roadside verge was filled with locals, walking along in single file. Some women carried baskets on their heads, using one hand to balance the load. There were men too, dressed in work clothes, on their way to nearby farms. The fields adjacent to the road looked green and healthy, with crops of maize, yams, and bananas. In places, remnants of forest looked to have been spared the axe and more than once we crossed over small bridges, which spanned busy streams of clear water.

Our guidebook also mentioned that the area was used for coffee plantations, but I didn't spot any from the minivan window and our driver's responses were getting harder to decipher. After forty minutes, the tarmac finished, and we merged with a wide, pitted track. Barefoot children ran alongside the minivan, waving and smiling as we made our way through the village towards the official starting point. As soon as our feet touched the ground, we were bombarded by a group of excited children. Each seemed to have a different product for sale. Some offered us chocolate, others called for us to purchase hats, T-shirts, or walking poles. With no other trekkers in sight, they were insistent on making a sale.

We loaded up on chocolate, but purchasing commemorative T-shirts before we'd even taken a step on the mountain seemed like tempting fate. The driver introduced us to Evans, our guide for the week. He was tall and muscular, with thick, dark hair under a red woollen hat–remarkably like the one that Oscar had worn, all those years ago.

I looked around, hoping he might be nearby, with another group of trekkers. But I stopped myself and snapped back to reality. It had been a long time ago, on another part of the mountain. Evans' voice was deep and the handshake a little too strong. His eyes didn't dwell on ours for long. Instead, they continually darted towards a group of local men, standing in the forest clearing. 'Wait here, please. I'll be back soon.'

Something was going on, but I couldn't quite grasp the situation. Evans walked purposefully towards the men and pointed to a few. He was handpicking porters. Those chosen ran over to the start line, to get instructions from a head porter. The ones left behind remained in the clearing, kicking the red dirt in frustration. I could sense their desperation, as there didn't seem to be many other walking parties around. More sellers approached, each with a hopeful smile, while holding up their wares. It was hard to say no and after a final sale I called out to Fran. 'We've now got three bars of chocolate each.'

Before we purchased any more, Evans appeared from the village, holding two plucked chickens and the freshly skinned leg of a large animal. It was probably part of a goat, but he still didn't seem to be in the mood for small talk.

While waiting for guidance from Evans, we watched the porters as they prepared the equipment. Tents, food and other essentials were wrapped in tarpaulins or placed in plastic containers. Some porters balanced loads on their heads, while others carried full loads on their backs. We stood awkwardly in the clearing while Evans barked instructions to his team, before racing off towards a group of nearby buildings.

'Are you sure we don't need walking poles? There's a lot for sale,' Fran muttered as we shunned another hopeful teenager standing close by. I stole a look at one of the hand-carved poles and said, 'Do you remember what the rep said last night, at the hotel bar? She was insistent that we wouldn't need them.'

'But they're only five dollars each, and once we leave here, there's no way to get any. What did you do when you climbed with Owen?'

I thought back to my previous time on the mountain, many years earlier. Some things were a blur, but the final assault up the steep scree suddenly came to mind. I'd fallen asleep while resting on a walking pole and had used it extensively during the steep descent from Gilman's Point. I smiled at Fran and said, 'I think our friend from last night is trying to trip us up. Mind you, I should know better. Come on, let's grab one each.'

The lad got his sale and ran off with our dollars, just as Evans appeared on the scene and ushered us towards the official starting point. Nearby, we discovered a stall selling water, snacks and walking poles. Some poles on display had the words *British Rail*, stamped across them. The seller didn't seem to know how he'd ended up with them, but they looked sturdy enough. I'd once heard that during the winter of 1991, parts of the British railway network ground to a halt, because of severe snowstorms. Maybe some of the disgruntled passengers had been given walking poles to help them in the drifts and had then travelled to Africa to climb Kilimanjaro!

Any type of snow is welcome these days on the summit. The glaciers found near the peak have been receding for decades, with experts divided on the reason. Some have melted away, never to return. Apart from global warming, another theory points to the deforestation on the lower slopes (now known as the cultivation zone). Some believe that with fewer trees there is a reduction in air moisture, which reduces cloud cover. We need clouds for rain and if it isn't raining, then it must be sunny and warm!

If the ice melt continues, there will come a time when the snows of Kilimanjaro will no longer shimmer over the African plains. It is estimated that since the early 1900s, Kilimanjaro has lost 80% of its ice. For some trekkers, the lack of a glacier or snow may be just a lost photo opportunity. For those who rely on seasonal meltwater for crops and livestock, the effects could be devastating. Wildlife will also be affected, if the streams dry up.

Alongside the walking pole entrepreneur was a stall that sold gaiters. These waterproof leggings attach over your lower legs and boots, to keep your feet dry when tackling muddy or damp terrain. Some instinct told me that the representative at the hotel last night was not giving the best advice. While we were in negotiation for two pairs, Evans appeared by our side. 'Listen carefully, mister Ali and wifey Fran. There has been lots of rain on the mountain. Today's trek will be boggy and energy sapping. Take your time and use your walking poles.'

While we sat to put on our gaiters, Evans urged us to hurry, as he was keen to make a move. As soon as we were on our feet, Evans called out that it was time to go. He then set off from base camp and headed into the jungle. We followed in close pursuit and soon found ourselves on a wide, boggy trail, surrounded by greenery and filled with strange noises. There were trees so tall it was hard to see where they ended, and others with complex root systems that threatened to trip us as we ploughed through the mud. From up ahead, Evans turned to face us and called out for attention. 'Mister Ali, please remember to walk poli-poli.'

Fran looked momentarily confused as I smiled at the memory of my first Kilimanjaro trek. 'Poli-poli, means slowly-slowly. He's telling us to slow down and enjoy the ride.'

I had niggling worries that, just like before, I was unprepared for the rigours ahead. Although the three-month trip to South America had been exhilarating, it had also been physically challenging at times. I'd arrived back in England 15 kilograms lighter, with ten days to prepare for the trip to Africa. Alice, my sister, came to the rescue with offers of home-cooked meals each evening, followed by tasty desserts. By the time she tearfully waved us off from her doorstep, my ribs were no longer showing.

Now I was trudging along a boggy jungle path, with Fran trailing a few steps behind. The porters had raced ahead, somehow blitzing through the muddy terrain with ease. The path was clear but rarely stayed straight or level for long. With each turn, we slowly gained altitude. In places, the track steepened, and we were forced to reach out for tree roots to find a handhold. In flatter terrain, deep puddles formed across the main path, which meant a diversion to locate drier ground.

Sometimes I spotted boot imprints from earlier walkers, embedded into dried patches of mud. Where were these people now? Had they made it to the top, like Dave and Paul, all those years ago? Or did they also succumb to altitude sickness and get escorted from the crater rim?

After numerous treks in the jungles of South America, I felt at home in the forest. Unlike the wide-open plains of the Serengeti, the wildlife that lives on the lower slopes of Kilimanjaro has many trees to hide behind. With time and patience, we were able to spot monkeys, high in the canopy and far from the track. We soon learned that diverting from the boggy path to find firmer footing, took up valuable time and strength. There was no point tiptoeing any longer. A frontal attack along the main trail proved to be the best option.

Apart from faraway sightings of monkeys and close encounters with buzzing insects, the only other wildlife we spotted was a multitude of differing birds. Mostly, they darted past or stayed high in the canopy. During one water stop, Fran spotted an inquisitive sunbird, strikingly blue against the green canopy, watching us from the safety of a branch. By late afternoon, the lush forest gradually receded, and the surrounding trees began to wither in size. We'd moved from one climate zone to another and soon came across a wide clearing, where Evans stood waiting. He opened his arms wide and called out, 'Welcome to the first camp, mister Ali and wifey Fran.'

Three dome tents flapped gently in the late afternoon breeze, with two camping stools and a fold-up table placed in the clearing. Evans showed us our home, a well-used but functional two-man tent, and didn't mention anything about sharing.

'When you are ready, there is popcorn waiting,' he murmured, leaving us alone to unpack our luggage, which had been transported by the porters. While dressed in fleeces and woollen hats, we devoured the popcorn, followed by a hot meal of goat stew and rice, served on the table outside. The light was fading fast, but a kerosene lamp helped with the last of the meal. By the time we'd finished, the mist and clouds had lifted, allowing our first view of the distant summit, sitting under a blanket of emerging stars. The only sound was laughter, coming from the cook's tent.

Evans appeared by our tent a while later, holding two mugs of steaming Milo. He handed them over with a bright smile and wished us good night. He'd lost the gruffness of the morning and was turning into a hospitable guide. The porters seemed to keep their distance despite my efforts at conversation, but managed to conjure up warm and tasty meals.

A few hours later, while lying next to Fran in the darkened tent I nudged her gently and said, 'I have a funny feeling we're going to make it to the top.'

'Do you really think so?' she asked sleepily.

'Yes, I honestly do. By the way, how's your sleeping bag?'

'It's nice and cosy, thanks. Why do you ask?'

'Oh nothing, just that mine feels too thin.'

There was no reply. Just her gentle breathing as I lay wide awake, thinking back to the frantic dash around the local shopping centre the day before we'd flown to Africa. Fran had chosen a four-season sleeping bag, reduced by ten pounds for three days only. My mind was obviously on other things at the time; I'd somehow left the store with a two-season sleeping bag, designed for summer camping trips.

I tried pushing away all thoughts of the last-minute shopping spree and turned my attention to the porter's laughter, drifting across the campsite. Their voices slowly faded, replaced by a soft wind buffeting the sides of the tent. Sleep, when it came, sucked me into a deep, obscure dream, involving a race to the frozen summit while being chased by the woman from the bar, demanding her 80 dollars. Her stilettos snapped on the ice, but she picked them up and chased me round the crater's edge. Owen also appeared in the dream, slouched against a snow-clad boulder with his Macmillan T-shirt. He smiled and waved as I raced past, in search of the top.

I woke with a start and opened my eyes. Sunlight brushed against the canvas but offered little warmth at such an early hour. I reached out for a hat and heard Fran's voice. 'Ali, are you awake?'

'Just about, but I've just had a weird dream and it's too cold to get up.'

She tried stirring me into action with a gentle nudge. 'I really need to go to the toilet. Will you come with me?'

I snuggled deeper into the sleeping bag and dropped my voice to a whisper. 'I'm finally feeling warm and would rather stay here.'

Her pitch changed immediately, bordering on desperation. 'Don't be silly. I'm bursting to go and don't know the way.'

'What time is it?' I asked.

'I've no idea. I just need the toilet, that's all.'

She then unzipped the tent door and opened the flap wide. From the comfort of my sleeping bag, I had a commanding view of Kibo, far in the distance, its snowy pinnacle bathed in early morning sunshine. Eager to capture the moment with a photo, I hastily dressed and stepped outside, just in time to catch sight of Fran racing across the mountainside, a fresh roll of toilet paper streaming behind her.

The long-drop toilet was hidden from view by a simple wooden structure, located close to the side of the track. Luckily for Fran it was unoccupied, and while she completed her business, I stared up at the summit, my thoughts on the climbers who now stood on the roof of Africa.

Too High

"The best way to make your dreams come true is to wake up."
Paul Valery

It didn't take long before Evans enquired about the music I was listening to while we walked that morning. By now, we'd left the forest, but were still surrounded by greenery. Instead of majestic trees, misty pathways and the high-pitched shrill of insects, we'd entered a heathery landscape, dotted with the same type of giant lobelia that I'd seen so many years before with Owen. We were on a different side of the mountain, but the similarities were hard to ignore.

I handed the music player to Evans, explained the playlist, and let him take his pick. He studied the options for a few seconds and then said, 'I think I will start with this one, mister Ali. I have never heard of a band called The Proclaimers, but a song that talks about walking 500 miles must be good.' He inserted the earphones, turned up the volume, and while humming along with the tune, led the way to the next camp.

Each night, the temperature continued to fall. Fran reacted by adding more layers before wriggling into her sleeping bag. Unfortunately, I couldn't do the same. Sleeping naked was a hard habit to shake, as pyjamas, jumpers and thermals have always brought me out in a heat rash. Fran reckoned I was like a hot water bottle; always warm, despite the season.

During the middle of the third night, I knew the habit had to change. I woke in the darkness, shivering violently. The cheap sleeping bag was no match for the freezing night-time temperatures. I groped for my discarded clothes in the dark and hastily donned them, before climbing into the cool sleeping bag. Fatigue knocked me out. I woke just before dawn, subconsciously scratching my inflamed arms. The clothes were ripped off again, allowing my blood to cool while I fidgeted on the sleeping mat, waiting for first light.

Our dome tent was coated in a thin layer of ice, which cracked as we unzipped the doorway and emerged into the chilled air. The campsite was sugar-coated in a veneer of shiny crystals. As the sun poked through the valley, Evans greeted us with tin mugs, filled with hot, sweet tea, which we held tightly while staring up at the mountaintop. The porters were relaxed as this was an acclimatisation day, so the tents could remain where they were. The plan was to ascend at a steady pace all morning, then return to Karanga camp by early afternoon.

Evans disappeared into the distance with my music and earphones for company. This allowed us time to trek alone across the alpine desert. The peak of the snow-capped summit was now in full view, silently calling for our attention as we clambered higher. Evans was waiting at the next rise, eyes closed, miming along with a song. He was joined by a porter and as we approached, he raised his voice and called out. 'Mister Ali, I like the song about walking 500 miles, but it is not good for walking poli-poli.'

Then he changed conversation and pointed to a wide slab of rock, laden with snacks and water. 'Sit for lunch, my friends, and enjoy the view. In a few days, I will guide you to the top of Kilimanjaro.'

While we nibbled on biscuits and took photos of the mountaintop, Evans sat nearby, working his way through the rest of the songs. During our descent to camp, he stopped by the trail, pulled out the earphones and waited as we drew nearer. 'Mister Ali, I like your taste in songs. But there is one tune that troubles me a little. Why does the singer want to die before he gets old? I hope he climbs Kilimanjaro before he does. Please give him my name and I will guide him to the roof of Africa.'

He popped in the earphones, flashed another bright smile, and headed into camp, humming the words to 'My Generation'. On our return, more tents had appeared and after a few hours' rest we joined our new neighbours for sundowners. The sun slipped behind the dormant volcano of Mount Meru, 70 kilometres to our west, as we exchanged stories under a velvet sky.

Fran was unusually quiet, rubbing her eyes between delicate sips of warm tea. She hadn't made any fuss or complaint since leaving the forest and I felt very proud of her, but each day was different, and I could sense fatigue setting in. 'I'm off to bed,' she whispered.

'Okay. See you soon. I won't be long.'

I moved away from the newcomers to gaze at a kaleidoscope of warm colours, caressing the snows of Kilimanjaro. A few minutes later, Evans appeared from the scrub and stood alongside me. 'What can you see, mister Ali?'

I took a deep breath, inhaling cool, crisp air as my eyes adjusted to the fading light. Dusk had crept silently across East Africa. The vast plains were plunging into darkness, but far below, the lights of Machame village could be clearly seen, hugging the base of the mountain. Narrow streaks of cloud trailed across the evening sky, losing their colour as the sky began to darken. I turned to Evans and pointed towards the distant lights. 'Well, I can see your village in the valley. There are also a few clouds to enjoy. Plus, I can see the snows of Kilimanjaro.'

'Yes, of course. Everyone looks at the snow, and yes, that is my beautiful village. But clouds, I do not see. They, mister Ali, are small bubbles that will soon float away. Tonight, there will be no clouds in the sky and do you know what that means?'

'Lots of stars.'

He let out a chuckle and said, 'Yes, bwana, there will be many bright stars. But tonight, I think you will be too cold to enjoy them, as it will get down to minus five degrees. Maybe even minus ten. I hope you and wifey have enough thermals. Good night, bwana.'

Although he ambled towards his tent, I raced back to mine. 'Fran, I think I made the wrong choice at the camping shop!'

'What are you on about?' came a mumbled reply. She was wearing thermals, socks and a woolly hat, while wrapped snugly in her sleeping bag.

'Evans just told me it might be minus ten tonight. I'm not spending another night freezing my nuts off. There's a change of plan. Tonight, I'm in with you.'

She sat upright, her headtorch illuminating the cramped tent. 'Ali, we're halfway up a mountain and I'm too tired for sex.'

'This isn't about sex, it's about survival. I'm serious. You know my sleeping bag is too thin for this type of weather.'

'Why don't you just wear extra layers?'

'I did last night and it wasn't enough. Plus, it sent my arms into an itching frenzy. If I stay naked and join you, my body temperature will be perfect. I know this plan will work.'

'You can do what you want, but I think you're delirious. I really need to sleep.'

She then closed her eyes and pulled the sleeping bag tight across her body. In the silence that followed, I grabbed my toothbrush and headed outside. As predicted by Evans, the clouds were dispersing. While brushing my teeth, I studied the milky trail of stars stretching across the night sky. I wanted to stay longer, but a biting wind tore into my clothes and stung my face. Instead, I switched on my headtorch before dashing back to the tent.

Once inside, I hastily shed my clothes and called for Fran to move over. There was no reply, only her shallow breathing. There was nothing to do but try to squeeze in without disturbing her. She stirred slightly as I wriggled in with a determined burst, cramming my arms into the tight gap until we were firmly sealed.

I relaxed and lowered my head, but instead of melting into a soft pillow my ear scraped against the floor. I craned my neck to scan the tent with my headtorch. My travel pillow had moved during the earlier wriggle. It was tantalisingly close, and I could just make out the *Made in China* label. Fran stirred and began to mumble. 'What are you doing? Please stop moving.'

My only option was to wait until she slept before reaching for the pillow. As expected, the temperature in our shared sleeping bag rose quickly. So too, did the urge to scratch my arms, which were now pinned by my sides. Soon, my body was stuck in two temperature zones. Below the neck, I was back in the jungles of South America, feeling hot, sticky, and itchy. Above the neck, I could feel the cool night air, promising frost within the hour. My woollen hat had somehow gotten lost, which meant my bald head was resting on the cold, hard floor. I knew my ears were turning blue but couldn't reach out to rub them.

Fatigue robbed me of any further plans to wriggle for the pillow and discarded hat, as I fell into a deep sleep. Hours later, I woke in darkness, feeling the shock of cold air on my weary face. My torch battery had died, and my pinned arms screamed for cool air. I needed to escape, but didn't want to wake Fran. Our bodies must have expanded in the heat, as I couldn't budge, which forced me to rock sideways to gain momentum.

We rolled, and suddenly I was free. Floundering naked in the freezing tent, I groped wildly until my fingers found the cheap sleeping bag, discarded in the corner. Where was my cosy hat? The tent was only a few metres wide, but the cold and dark hampered my search. Fran always arranged the tent neatly. 'Everything has its place,' she would tell me time and time again.

She seemed to know the location of every essential item. If only I'd taken notice, as I was now groping blindly for any layers I could find. Within minutes, I was wrapped snugly in three T-shirts, thermals and a hat. I climbed into the sleeping bag, pulled it tight around my body and snuggled up against Fran. Blood flowed to my ear lobes as they rested on the lost pillow. My hat felt weird, but sleep came quickly.

Fran's giggles woke me. Daylight streamed through the tent as she emerged from her winter hibernation and studied me with a quizzical look. As I rubbed my eyes and sat up straight, she asked, 'Why are you wearing underpants on your head?'

Any remaining lethargy was shaken away by strong coffee and the promise of a steep section of scrambling, later in the morning. As the exposed crag appeared, I looked down into the valley. It was scattered with small settlements surrounded by remnants of emerald forest. By now we'd climbed to over 4,000 metres, towards an area known as the Karanga valley. Later, we were thankful for the band of heavy clouds that rolled across the sky, to halt the falling temperatures.

Each evening, just after dinner, Evans would appear at our tent door for a quick chat about the next day's plan. Today he did the same, but this time his expression looked tense. 'I hope you are happy with the food and service that my porters constantly provide. They are the best men in the village. But you must understand, we get paid very little and the *jifty* is very important to us. The additional money will help us feed our families and educate our children.'

He seemed eager to tell us more and sat on one of the camp chairs to get comfortable. 'As you know, there are two guides, one cook and three porters, all helping you to reach the summit. Please do not insult us with handshakes and a few coins at the end. Let us all be happy with the jifty.'

After the brief speech, his smile returned. 'In the morning, we will break camp and head to Barafu. Tomorrow night, I will guide you to the roof of Africa.'

As he walked away, Fran turned towards me and asked, 'What's a jifty?'

'I think it's his word for a tip and we've got two days to figure out the going rate.'

The following morning, we set off on the four-hour trek to Barafu campsite, located far below the crater at 4,680 metres. As instructed by Evans, we maintained a poli-poli rhythm across the wide-open plateau, passing a few hardy shrubs clinging to the dry soil. Our plan was to have an early dinner and a few hours' sleep until Evans woke us for the final ascent at midnight. Surprisingly, we both slept well, until woken from deep dreams by Felix, our assistant guide.

Fran had meticulously prepared our clothes and we were soon scrambling to get into thermal layers and fleeces. The early start plus the confines of the tent and intense cold hampered our efforts. Evans was getting impatient, as timing was essential to reach the summit at dawn. Just as I left the tent, my headtorch refused to work. There were spare batteries located somewhere in my belongings, but finding them quickly would be difficult.

Luckily, the moon was high and offered a natural source of illumination. Felix took up the rear guard and the four of us left camp. We trekked at a slow, methodical pace, silently inching our way under a blaze of stars. Despite the early hour, I fought for every breath. As a distraction, I focused on Evans' boots, as they bit into the loose gravel.

Sometime later, I heard voices coming from the path below. We halted by the edge of the track to allow a group of trekkers to pass by. Within minutes, they'd been swallowed up by the night. I was amazed at their speed but knew the dangers of moving quickly, this close to the summit. I called out in the darkness, but my words sounded croaky and muffled. 'What time is it, Evans?'

'It's two o'clock, mister Ali.'

My mind raced. Two hours gone, four more to go, and my legs were already wobbling. I thought back to the time with Owen. At least this time, I wasn't coughing. I looked around to see the shrunken figure of Fran, hidden deep under multiple layers and a thick woolly hat. Her eyes seemed glazed, but it was hard to tell in the darkness. Just before we set off, I reached out for her hands. 'You're doing great. How are you feeling? Are the gloves warm enough?'

In response, I got a mumbled reply. 'What time is it? Are we there yet? Water, please.'

Our bottles were freezing up, but a dribble of icy water eased her cracked lips. After a swift drink, she tried speaking, but her voice sounded low and croaky. 'What time is it, please?'

'It is time to go,' was the curt reply from Evans.

The next stop came quicker. By now it was just after three and Evans explained we were halfway to Stella Point, which marks the edge of the crater. Although I'd lost the feeling in my toes and couldn't shake off a pounding headache, I still felt strong.

I'd been watching Fran's progress during the last few hours and realised she was digging deep. Only now, in the pale light from the moon, could I see that she still had luminous foam plugs pushed firmly into her ears, from when she'd been sleeping. During one of our infrequent stops, I fiddled with her lobes in the darkness but got no response. She just sucked on a frozen water bottle, leaning against her trekking pole while staring into space, as I pulled out the earplugs.

Once again, Evans stirred us into action, calling for us to follow him along the steep path, which zig-zagged up the featureless slope. Mental strength kicked in as we plodded upwards without thought. Sometimes we stumbled in the dark or complained about the cold, but our gripes fell on deaf ears. Instead, we used every opportunity to take a break as we leaned on the walking poles and fought for breath. Fran began repeating the same question over and over. Each time she asked how long we had to go, the answers from Evans were too honest and not what we wanted to hear.

When possible, we glanced up at the forgotten stars, but despite their beauty we rarely stopped to admire them. Sometime later, reality drifted into dreamtime. For the second time in my life, I began sleepwalking on Kilimanjaro. I've no idea how many steps I took, before stumbling over Evans' boots and falling to the floor.

He helped me up and dusted me down, then urged me to keep moving, with the promise of something special very soon. We set off silently once more, trudging through the scree as though it was treacle. Just as I began to doubt his word, the first hint of light radiated from beyond the mountain, revealing the faint outline of what could only be the crater rim.

Evans came to a halt and declared we'd made it to Stella Point. I pulled Fran close for a hug, knowing that we were very close to the summit. Her eyes were clear and for the first time in many hours, she managed a weary smile. We took a break and gulped down warm tea from Felix's flask. He'd been at the rear all night, slowly prodding us forward with words of encouragement. Only now, while nearing our goal, did we comprehend and appreciate his efforts. There is no doubting that Evans and Felix had carefully nurtured our movements, ensuring we moved at the right pace, with just enough support.

We were close to the area where my first foray up the mountain had ended with a spectacular vomit onto rocks and snow. But as Evans stood and called us forward to the summit, we rose together and walked steadily along the frozen path. A cold blanket of mist drifted over our feet, following the gentle contours of the crater.

To our left stood the shining buttress of Furtwängler Glacier. Although much of the ice has melted since the pioneering days, it still looked formidable and made a perfect backdrop for an impromptu photo. As I huddled against Fran, Evans took a hurried photo of us in front of the mass of ice, standing five metres high. Soon after, we continued silently towards Uhuru Peak, where up ahead I noticed flags and a wooden post!

It was just after sunrise, and we were alone on the roof of Africa. Fran burst into tears of joy and I raised my hands high, smiling and thinking of my mum. We reached out for Evans and Felix, and then hugged them tight. Handshakes and grins at 5,895 metres. From my rucksack I pulled out a St George's flag and posed with Fran and the guides for a photo. It seemed hypocritical, as we were leaving England to live in Australia, maybe forever, but at the time it felt like the right thing to do.

After our brief ceremony and photo shoot, Evans was keen to depart. As I placed the flag back into my bag, more trekkers came into view, ending our brief solitude at the top. A desperate plea from another trekker halted our departure. His camera had frozen before he had the chance to take a photo.

I took a quick snap of him with my device, and while he scribbled his email address on a piece of paper, the sun cast a vast shadow of Kilimanjaro across the African plains. The spell was broken by muffled coughs from the path below, signalling a steady influx of exhausted trekkers, eager to reach the summit. I stuffed the piece of paper deep into my rucksack and began the descent.

We retraced our steps past the crater rim and then dropped back onto the mountainside. Initially, Evans led us away from the path, so that we didn't interfere with those still trekking to the top. Their contorted faces momentarily came to life as we shouted words of encouragement while heading past. Gravity, adrenalin and loose stones propelled us towards camp, until our tired legs buckled under the strain.

Evans called for a stop, and as we drained the last of the tea, he sat close by and gathered his thoughts for a speech. 'Well done, my friends. You have both stood proudly on the roof of Africa. I knew you would do it. Remember the jifty, please. Without my skills and knowledge, plus the help from the support crew, you would not have achieved your dreams. Tomorrow we will finish, and I'd like you to think about the jifty. Now we must go!'

We understood his point, but not the timing. We wouldn't run away without giving a worthy tip. He was either pushy or desperate. Maybe he'd been given poor tips previously and now took control early on. I forced the thought aside to concentrate on the steep path. We pushed lower until early afternoon, then flailed into camp, to find the porters in a huddle around their tent. On closer inspection, we could see that it was awkwardly skewed, because of a broken pole.

For a few moments Evans began shouting at the porters, his voice carrying far and filled with obscenities. After calming down, he strolled over to where I sat with Fran. He stood alongside and quietly asked if we'd write a letter, explaining that the pole had snapped in high winds. Otherwise, the money for the replacement part would have to come from their wages. Our thoughts turned to the woman we'd met at the hotel bar, who was part of the family that owned this trekking company. Her world was a far cry from the local tribes, slogging it out on the mountain to feed their families.

Our final breakfast was taken in bright sunshine. We gazed at the twin peaks of Mawenzi and Kibo, finally allowing the euphoria and accomplishment to wash over us. The close encounter with the summit a decade earlier had often been in my thoughts, as I'd vowed to reach the top in memory of my mum. I now felt thankful for the second opportunity to complete this wish.

At the time of her passing, I was 24 years of age. With each year, the memories of life with her were fading. But after the excitement of reaching the summit I somehow felt reconnected, as if she knew. Once again, I could remember those special times, when we shared laughs and cups of tea in our family kitchen.

By early afternoon, we emerged from the forest into a village, where a group of children sat together by a stream. As we approached, they noisily bounded towards us, carrying buckets of water and scrubbing brushes. While they cleaned our boots, a barrage of questions came our way.

'Did you reach the top, bwana?'

'Did you touch the snow? I bet it was very cold.'

'Where are you from?'

'Are you married?'

'How many children do you have?'

'Would you like a T-shirt? My brother has the best ones for sale.'

With clean boots, we tipped the smiling children and ambled lower, seeking the T-shirt sellers that waited patiently in line along the trail.

With the sun on our backs, it was time to head to Zanzibar, but not before our guides and porters got their well-earned tip and a signed letter, concerning a stormy night on the mountain. Evans counted the US dollars methodically and then recounted them again. Finally, he looked up and gave a sheepish grin. 'Thank you, mister Ali and wifey Fran. My team is waiting to go home and will be happy with their jifty.'

A brief, firm handshake and he was gone. The porters were waiting and crowded round for a fast exchange of notes, handshakes, and high fives. While back at the hotel, I emailed the climber that I met on the summit, with a photo attached. Soon after, I swam with Fran in the hotel pool and together we watched storm clouds gather over the mountain. Just after sunset, we enjoyed pre-dinner drinks at the bar. The same barman was on hand to serve us and while preparing Fran's gin and tonic, he congratulated us on reaching the top. During dinner, we feasted on Indian curries and Kilimanjaro beer, as the restaurant roof quivered from the rain.

Kilimanjaro Porters

A Poo with a View

Lost and Found

"If you want to see the sunshine, you have to weather the storm."
Frank Lane

While taking a stroll outside the hotel the following morning, the extent of the overnight storm became clear. The clouds were gone, revealing a fresh layer of welcome snow across Kibo and the surrounding slopes. The glimmering summit looked impossibly white against the hazy blue of the African sky and got me thinking about those who had set off at midnight to reach the top. Did they have to trudge through deep snow, just like Hans Meyer, all those years ago?

After waving goodbye to the friendly barman, we headed into Moshi by taxi, then boarded a bus to take us overland towards the coast. With each turn in the road, the mountain dwindled from view. I kept looking through the bus windows for glimpses of the snowy summit, but all too soon it was gone, and our Kilimanjaro adventure was over. I was then lulled to sleep while gazing at the surrounding fields and rolling hills, wondering if I'd ever be lucky enough to return someday. Hours later, Fran prodded me awake. The fields were gone, replaced by busy streets, filled with cars and people.

After the laid-back vibe of Moshi, we were unprepared for the fast pace of Dar es Salaam, the country's largest city. Our aim was to get to the spice island of Zanzibar, 70 kilometres offshore. To earn this reward meant circumnavigating the travel agents, hawkers, and merchants located along a thin strip near the water's edge. The harbour was filled with an assortment of vessels, including traditional wooden dhows, modern passenger ferries and cargo ships.

As we approached the row of makeshift cabins, a wave of smiling black faces descended. They crowded around us, each with a story to tell or something to sell. A thin teenager was first to speak. 'Please, bwana, come with me. I will take you to the ferry.'

From the back of the group, another voice called out for attention. 'Over here! Please look. I have spare tickets for the ferry but be quick as it leaves in a few minutes.'

With so many options and a lack of personal space, we needed to gather our thoughts. I smiled politely and took hold of Fran's hand as we eased our way through the eager crowd. They stepped away, holding tickets up high and calling for our attention. Twenty steps later, we faced the same scenario. The strip was full of hopeful sellers and all eyes were on us. We edged to the window of the nearest shop, hoping to find special deals on display, but all we saw were our own wilted reflections.

There was no space to think. We turned from the window to find the hawkers still looming. Tickets were thrust into our hands with promises of an imminent departure, but an open door at the nearest ticket office offered the chance to escape. The smiling owner greeted us from the counter, sweating slightly despite the wide fan whirring from the ceiling. 'I'm glad you have found my tourist information centre. You did the right thing by avoiding those people outside.'

It was only now, that I noticed his hands. He was continually rubbing them together, while speaking in a slow, assured manner. 'Now, sir, what can I do for you? Are you after a safari experience? I know the best guides in Tanzania. Or maybe you want to trek to the top of Kilimanjaro.'

'No thanks. We're just after two ferry tickets to Zanzibar, please.'

'Yes, of course. I can arrange that easily enough. What time tomorrow, would you like to leave?'

'We want them for this afternoon, please. A man out there said—'

'I am sorry, bwana. Those men are not professionals and shouldn't be believed. The ferries have stopped, but I can get you to the island another way. I have two tickets left for this afternoon's flight, at a special price for you.'

'Flight. Did you say flight?'

'Yes, of course. There is an airport nearby and we will fly you in comfort across the water. The view is beautiful from up high. Do you need accommodation as well? I can get you the best deal for any of the hotels.'

I was beginning to doubt his credentials and contemplated walking away. A glance at the men gathered close to the doorway convinced me to stay put a little longer. Fran guided me to the corner of the shop and in whispers we confirmed our plan. The man watched while we spoke and was still standing by the counter when we returned. 'We don't need accommodation, thanks, as we're eager to be as flexible as possible. As for the flight, we hadn't planned for this. How much will it cost?'

He grabbed a calculator and tapped a few numbers into it. 'My special price for you both, will be 80 US dollars.'

'How much is that, compared to the ferry?'

'There is no ferry today, mister, so it is not worth thinking about. Besides, air travel is far quicker and only a little more expensive. Please, do not waste my time anymore. Already it is getting late and the last flight will soon be taking off. If you want to be sipping beers in Zanzibar tonight, I suggest you act quickly.'

Feeling that we had no other choice, we paid the dollars into his open palm. He quickly checked the money and gave a satisfied nod. 'Thank you, bwana. I will order a taxi to take you to the airport. Please wait here.'

Fran stayed in the office with the rucksacks while I headed outside. The sellers by the doorway sensed we'd made a sale and slowly dispersed. I then saw a man approaching. He was wide built, with a deep tan, tattooed arms and shoulder length hair, styled into dreadlocks. He looked to be in his mid-thirties and had the easy gait of someone that had travelled far and wide. While passing by, he casually asked, 'Hey man, are you on the next ferry to Zanzibar? It's leaving soon.'

As we stood together in the late sunshine, he explained about the various ferry companies that operated from the harbour. The agents didn't sell tickets for every crossing, so it was essential to shop around. If we wanted to reach Zanzibar by boat, the adjacent shop was selling the last few tickets. Then he pointed to the street sellers and said, 'Or you can ask those men as well. They usually have tickets on hand, but be careful with showing your money in public.'

I thanked the man and returned to the shop. Inside, I came face to face with the grinning owner, alongside our taxi driver. Flushed with anger, I headed to the counter and called to Fran to grab her bag. She looked over quizzically, but I kept my stare on the agent, who was now losing his smile.

'I've just heard about a shop nearby that is selling tickets for a sunset crossing. I don't want your plane tickets and just want our money back.'

'It is too late, bwana. I have the flight tickets and the taxi is waiting.'

I moved near enough to see the first flecks of grey in his slicked hair. 'We're not getting in the taxi or accepting the plane tickets. I'd like a refund, please. There's a ferry leaving soon, and we plan to be on it. I don't appreciate being lied to.'

I was expecting some type of showdown, but he shrugged his shoulders and returned our money without a word. Within an hour, we were sitting on the deck of a modern catamaran, skimming across the Indian Ocean towards Zanzibar. Our destination was the historical port of Stone Town, basking in the late sunshine.

Those seeking fortune or adventure have been drawn to the island for centuries. It was here that Livingstone stayed before his trek into the African interior, in search of the source of the Nile. During his time on the island, he witnessed the suffering and greed of human trafficking, with thousands of slaves arriving in Zanzibar each year during the mid-19th century. They lived in squalor and were paraded at outdoor markets, before being sold to work in clove and coconut plantations or exported to the Middle East for a life of misery. Thankfully, the slave trade in Zanzibar ended in 1873, after the signing of a treaty by the Sultan.

Nowadays, Zanzibar is renowned for its exotic spices, as it has the ideal climate for growing nutmeg, pepper and cloves. These are exported across the world and the demand is always high. The island has many other attributes, including its friendly people, warm weather, tropical beaches and pristine coral reefs. Stone Town has lots to offer, including a labyrinth of cobbled laneways and ancient harbourside houses, each with a story to tell. With a spring in our step, we stepped off the boat, expecting to be swarmed with offers of help.

Unlike the touts who'd harassed us on the mainland, the small gathering of locals at the quayside seemed far less pushy. No one called out loudly or stood too close to gain our attention. A teenager with a cheeky grin caught our eye and offered to help Fran with her rucksack. We then set off with him towards a hostel that he knew. He'd get a commission and we'd get a room with a ceiling fan and an air conditioner. The small, family-run place he chose for us was located along a narrow street, and during the walk he continually took shortcuts through unnamed alleyways.

Our room was clean and simple, and the ceiling fan worked perfectly. The air conditioner kicked to life when switched on, but for all its groans, did little to stir the sultry air. It was time to get out and explore. Although we didn't have a map of the area, I doubt it would have helped. The humidity, heat and constant distractions added to the mix, to create a vibrant atmosphere with endless possibilities to happily get lost in the warren of alleyways and cobbled backstreets.

Stone Town moves at a different pace to most of the Western world. Ambling slowly, we came across intricate doorways carved with meticulous care, now fading with age. Houses and apartments were alive with laughter, as the zesty aroma of spices drifted in the balmy night air. Our aim was to exit this maze at the quayside, where each evening the locals come to enjoy freshly cooked seafood and spicy delights.

After many dead ends, we spotted an unlit alleyway and tried our luck. A few steps later, we emerged into a bustling night market, next to the water's edge. Anchored dhows clinked gently in the harbour, waiting patiently for dawn. Kerosene lamps were being lit by the vendors, casting a soft glow across the ancient harbour walls. We shared our meal of succulent king prawns, grilled kingfish and chapati with an inquisitive cat. With each portion, he moved nearer, until we could reach out and stroke his soft black coat.

As the cat jumped onto the sea wall for a nap, my eyes were drawn to a white-faced family walking amongst the Arabs and Africans. I was keen to chat and discovered they were from Switzerland, having travelled throughout the year by sailboat. Their youngest of just four years stood munching on a prawn kebab, while his older sister by two years, sat and devoured a grilled chapati. I felt proud of the parents for embarking on such an epic journey and giving their children the kind of experiences that could last a lifetime.

Our ambles back to the hostel were different each evening, as we always got lost. Not once did we ever feel threatened, no matter where we went or who we met. During another humid evening, we encountered a huge Arab, dressed in a bright white, flowing robe. He was standing in the shadows of an alley and for a moment I thought we'd walked onto the set of an Indiana Jones movie shoot! He stood to one side, his robe flapping gently in the welcome breeze. As our paths crossed, he smiled brightly and gently called out, 'Jambo,' as he slid past us into the night.

The following evening, we followed the advice in our guidebook, hoping to watch the sunset while sipping cool drinks. Our destination was Africa House, a prominent landmark with a chequered history of ownership, ranging from wealthy slave traders to the first English Club in East Africa. It is now a hotel, and because of its colonial past and enviable location on the waterfront, remains a popular haunt for those seeking sundowners.

During our stroll towards the hotel, it seemed many of the tourists staying in Stone Town had similar ideas to us. They appeared out of alleyways and from the beachfront, mostly young couples, all with the same destination in mind. Two more joined the road, popping out of a clothing shop, and then finding their bearings before merging with the flow of foot traffic. Some had street maps to help with navigation. Others boldly forged ahead, eager to arrive in time for the spectacle.

Luckily, we'd timed our arrival perfectly and nabbed the last seats on the veranda of the Sunset Bar. Eager staff members were on hand, to take orders and deliver drinks, while all eyes settled on the setting sun, edging its way to the milky horizon. For all the ambience and charm, I felt edgy and fidgety. Something didn't seem right, and I wanted to escape from the crowd.

Sunsets don't always have to be about the colour of the sky. Instead of watching the sun drop towards the ocean, I suddenly felt the urge to experience life in Stone Town, during the transition from day to night. Fran didn't agree, as we'd just secured panoramic seats and she was now settled with a cocktail, in anticipation of a memorable sunset. With a promise to return soon, I requested another cocktail from a passing waitress, planted a kiss on Fran's cheek and made a dash for the stairs.

I raced down two at a time, sidestepping the latecomers, and within a few minutes, was lost in Stone Town. I ran until my heart pounded in my ears. First right, then left, through an alleyway, left again, blindly heading into the labyrinth. The rush subsided, and I slowed down to find a suitable place to stop. By now, I was partway through a narrow backstreet. Just ahead lay a scattering of houses, overlooking a cobbled plaza. I sat with my camera and waited patiently, despite the continual buzzing of mosquitoes.

A slender girl, dressed in a black robe, appeared from the shadows, oblivious to my presence as she raced past on her way home. Then a young lad on a homemade scooter came down the alleyway, singing gently as he trundled along, during the last fragments of daylight. A woman opened a carved door and stepped into the street to call her children. She wore a dark shawl that fell to her ankles and as she called again, her eyes met mine. In response, I lowered my camera, just as two children arrived on the scene. After ushering them inside, she smiled and waved at me, before closing the door.

Soon after, a man strolled past and gave me a tired smile. He was pushing a wooden cart, which was now empty after a day's work. He wore a long green robe and sandals, which kicked up dust with each of his laboured steps. Then I spotted a black cat, lurking in the shadows, as though it was stalking some unseen prey.

Moments later, a young boy raced home, whistling a tune as he ran past me into his front yard. The door to his house slammed shut, leaving the darkened alleyway in silence. By now, the mosquitoes were biting and the street had grown silent. I found my bearings and walked towards the waterfront, thinking back to the small, but intimate moments I'd just witnessed.

'You missed a stunning sunset,' Fran reminded me with a knowing smile, as I strolled into the lively bar. I returned her smile and called for a cold beer and another cocktail. Together, we watched the stars emerge, while sharing our different experiences of a sunset in Zanzibar.

The following morning, we headed for Kendwa, a village that has grown from a series of fishing shacks, into a premier beach destination. For two days, we lodged close to the ocean and enjoyed the party atmosphere of a beachside bar. We also took an excursion into the interior with a local guide, to learn about the spice trade and to sample some of the produce.

We then moved to the east of the island and found ourselves a beachside hut in the welcoming fishing village of Jambiani, perched delicately alongside the white sands. The pristine environment lifted our spirits and we soon settled into a relaxed pace of life. Sometimes we'd sit on the balcony, watching children cycle along the beach on their way to school, or we'd wander down to the shoreline to watch fishermen arrive with their catch of the day. After a few days, we heard about the chance to snorkel alongside dolphins, in a location called Menai Bay, which could be reached by boat from the fishing village of Kizimkazi.

Rather than being part of a tour group on a bus, which picked up from hostels across the island each morning, we decided to beat the pack by hiring a motorbike and riding straight to the marina. Despite the early hour, each boat owner was up and about, preparing for the minibuses that would soon deposit hordes of eager tourists. We struck a deal with the owner of a small, powered craft and climbed on board. He was keen to depart as quickly as possible, so that he could return to the marina to collect more tourists before the wind picked up.

The early departure would have paid off, but sad grunts from the outboard motor delayed us. Perseverance, an oily rag and plenty of WD40 seemed to work the necessary magic. The motor coughed to life, just as the first minibus of the day appeared by the dockside, filled with tourists. Our captain seemed keen to make up for lost time and crashed through a series of waves, as we headed to deeper waters.

As the boat slowed, he pointed to a container in the hull, filled with snorkelling equipment, and asked us to get ready. He turned the tiller so that we faced into the wind, then let the motor idle. We didn't quite appreciate his urgency until he called out, 'You need to be quick, as the dolphins could be here soon.'

I was having problems with finding matching fins, and Fran's mask looked to have been adjusted to fit a sumo wrestler. While she struggled with the straps, I hunted for some better equipment at the bottom of the container. Then the captain pointed to our left and called out, 'They are here. You must go now. Jump, jump.'

But Fran only had one fin attached and was still struggling with the mask strap. While she adjusted her kit, our captain watched the dolphins as they swam away. He then kicked the engine into life once more and gave chase. Minutes later, the dolphins were under our boat and the captain was hollering for us to get ready. Fran had pulled on the mask, but her eyes were hidden behind fogged lenses. The captain cut the engine and urged us to leap overboard.

We hit the water and looked all around, but the dolphins had vanished. The captain heaved us aboard and sped after them again. As we raced across the bay, he pointed towards a dorsal fin carving through the water. He slowed the craft, urging us to jump in as soon as he'd cut the engine.

I dived in deeply and checked the surroundings. All I could see were grey flashes and bubbles. Then nothing, all the way back to the surface. I spotted Fran, coughing and red-eyed, with the fogged-up goggles wrapped around her forehead. Our young captain bellowed from the boat, calling us to the side so he could pluck us from the water.

I finally realised that we'd been sucked into an *ecotourism* nightmare. Caught up in the chase, we'd lost all respect for the dolphins. After clambering back on board, we informed the captain that we wanted to head back to shore. We were ashamed to be part of it. The captain followed our wishes and turned back, just as the first official boats tore into view. Each was filled with waving tourists, their masks and snorkels already in place across tanned, smiling faces.

Back in Jambiani, we took a stroll along the shoreline to watch local women harvesting the nutrient-rich seaweed. An ingenious set of wooden traps collects the seaweed as it floats past on each high tide. They'd already collected enough to fill many straw baskets and still had more traps to investigate. The seaweed is in high demand and much of it is exported across the world, as far away as China. With only a day left in the area, it was time to catch our own supper, so we went in search of a fisherman.

'Have you tried Captain Rastaman?' suggested our hostel owner. 'He owns the type of dhow that we call a Ngalawa. It's a carved-out canoe with a sail and has an outrigger to keep it stable. It will be perfect for a trip to the reef and he claims to know a few secret spots.'

He pointed to a row of market stalls and gave us a description of Captain Rastaman. We spotted him at once, sitting with friends while quietly playing cards. He wore shorts, a singlet and a multi-coloured hat that was unable to contain his long dreadlocks. We negotiated a time and price and met him the following afternoon at the beach. He'd also convinced a newlywed couple to come along. Liam and Kate were both blonde and looked to be in their early thirties, with easy-going, Canadian accents. They were staying nearby, at an all-inclusive complex, and were keen to escape from the other honeymooners for a few hours.

After quick greetings, we helped push the narrow wooden boat from the beach and then climbed on board. Once we were freed from the shallows, Captain Rastaman hoisted the ivory coloured sail. It twitched and flapped until he found the correct angle and then blossomed into a tight curve.

We were soon joined by a pod of dolphins, as we made our way under a perfect blue sky towards a secret spot. Close to the reef, he turned the boat into the wind and it came to rest, as the sail deflated.

The dolphins dived below the surface and vanished from view, just as he threw in the anchor. We waited while he prepared a set of simple hand lines, each comprising a reel, fishing hook and tiny strips of calamari for bait. As the water lapped gently against the hull, I turned to the honeymooners. 'Would you like to go snorkelling? You can borrow our gear.'

They looked at each other for a moment too long and I could sense something was not quite right. Kate leaned near and whispered softly, 'I'd love to, but can't swim.'

She prodded her husband playfully in his prominent ribs. 'You go in. Don't let me stop you.'

Liam shook his head and replied, 'No, I'm good for now. I'll stay on board for a bit longer and help to catch supper.'

The sea was perfectly flat and crystal clear. I dived deep and kicked hard towards a forest of coral, filled with sea life. Schools of tiny zebra fish kept their distance, as I briefly entered their world. When my lungs complained, I headed for the surface. Fran floated nearby, her eyes hidden behind a steamed-up mask.

Captain Rastaman called us on board for a fishing lesson, before handing over the hand-lines and bait. He then sat back against the mast and pulled down his trademark hat, to shield his eyes from the sun. We lowered the baited lines into the water, and within 20 minutes, some of the zebra fish I'd earlier spotted were now swimming in a plastic bucket, filled with seawater. After an hour, we'd caught enough between us to make a packet of fish fingers.

Captain Rastaman woke a few times to stretch his long limbs and inspect our catch. He nodded sedately when we showed him the contents, then returned to sleep under the folded sail. As time slipped slowly by, the captain snoozed while we sat together, chatting and fishing. Each of us faced the same direction, towards the island of Zanzibar. From our vantage point, we could see palm trees swaying and a few distant clouds, floating harmlessly across the sky.

Whenever the humidity became too unbearable, we'd jump overboard to cool down, except for Kate. She stayed put, catching fish and laughing at her husband's jokes. Fran was the first to notice the change in the weather. She was swimming back to the boat and had a perfect view of the dark clouds, forming behind us.

I studied the water and realised that a subtle change had occurred on the surface, with ripples nudging the sides of our anchored dhow. A sudden breeze brushed against the boat, rocking it gently and tugging at the secured sails. The captain had created a makeshift bed under the mast, protected from the sun by a flap of sail. Fran clambered on board and called out for his attention. 'Have you seen the clouds? I think we need to head back.'

He poked his head up from below the sail and gave us a broad smile. 'Relax, lady, it's just a passing shower. Carry on fishing. Hakuna matata.'

As he ducked back under the sail, I studied the incoming clouds and let out an involuntary gasp. This wasn't just a shower, but a fully fledged weather system tearing down on us. Above the rumble of distant thunder, I called out to the captain. 'What are you doing? This isn't the time for sleeping! Pull up the anchor and we'll be back on land in a few minutes.'

His face appeared once more, and I pointed to the pale-faced honeymooners. 'She can't swim, and they're only just married!'

He smiled once again, then pulled the sail over his shoulders and turned away, seemingly oblivious to the claps of thunder that were getting louder by the minute. Out to sea, the iron-grey curtain loomed closer. By now, I realised that a break for the shore would prove disastrous for the boat and its passengers. We'd left it too late and needed to save ourselves. We'd soon be drinking the freshest water this side of the Kalahari, and lifejackets were an optional extra that we'd forgotten to sign for. The blackest clouds collided, followed by a streak of lightning, which ripped across the sky. The honeymooners were locked in an embrace, but I quickly formed a simple plan. 'When the storm hits, don't panic, or stand up, and bale like hell.'

Grabbing the bucket, I tossed the zebra fish to freedom and handed the empty container to the newlyweds. Fran found a tin bowl and I had my sun hat ready, as we waited silently for the assault. The storm punched hard, driving thick drops of horizontal rain across the bay, obliterating all chances of conversation as a chilly wind tore through our saturated clothes. Freak gusts whipped seawater over the sides of the dhow, triggering an automatic response for survival, as the hull began to fill.

A dark shadow cloaked the boat as we baled relentlessly, ignoring the rain that lashed against our faces. Despite our efforts, the water level continued to rise. We were sinking! Suddenly, the boat lurched unevenly. We turned as one and came face to face with our captain, crawling from his hideaway and holding a wooden bowl. Fran's arms moved with the speed of a clockwork drummer, scooping out each wave with a determined ferocity, and with all five of us in synchronisation the water in the dhow gradually subsided.

Just as quickly as it had arrived, the storm passed, and the wind eased. The sun made an appearance and the dark clouds continued on their way. Captain Rastaman declared the fishing trip was over, hoisted the sodden sail and followed the wake of the storm back to the island. Back on land we declined the offer of a sunset cruise and bade farewell to the captain and newlyweds.

We returned to Stone Town for our last night in Zanzibar, which gave me the chance to search for a tailor to mend my tattered trousers. There was a huge emotional attachment to this simple garment, worn out from climbing mountains and working in the Amazonian jungle. They'd become a symbolic part of the journey for me.

After we'd booked into a family run hostel, I enquired about a local tailor. The owner led us outside, pointed to a nearby alleyway, and told us to follow our nose. We found the tailor's workshop in a shady plaza, along with a welcome café and a selection of market stalls. In one corner, two elderly men sat opposite each other, both studying the pieces on a chessboard. The grey-haired tailor ran nimble fingers across the ripped and threadbare trousers, as he assessed the damage with professional ease. He then nodded slowly before naming his price. I paid up front, with the condition they'd be ready for collection within a few hours.

We decided to celebrate our last evening in Zanzibar with a visit to the harbourside food market. Fran was keen to try more of the king prawn kebabs, and I was looking forward to catching up with the resident cat. As we approached the harbour, we met a few tourists walking towards us. They'd been turned away, as a cholera scare had forced the area to be quarantined. One of them knew of a beachside restaurant close by and we were invited to join them. They were a mixed bunch of five Europeans, who'd met during an excursion a few days earlier and had remained in touch.

Ten minutes later, we were in an open plan restaurant, studying a seafood menu and ordering drinks. Instead of chairs, each of us lounged on soft cushions, which were scattered freely on woven mats. Ceiling fans offered the chance of a welcome breeze and somewhere in the background, the sound of Freddy Mercury helped set the scene. Someone mentioned that he'd once lived nearby, which steered the talk towards music and travel.

In the decadent surroundings, conversations flowed freely as we shared stories while tucking into spicy food and cool drinks. Sometime later, Fran told the group about our adventure on the high seas with Captain Rastaman. Others pitched in with humorous stories of their own and between bouts of laughter I settled into the deep cushions and closed my eyes. I must have nodded off, as the next thing I remember was someone nudging me. I opened my eyes and stared into Fran's smiling face. 'Ali, wake up, as we need to go. You've been dribbling.'

'What time is it?'

'It's nearly eleven. You've been asleep for an hour.'

I jolted upright. 'I forgot to collect my mended trousers, and we're leaving in the morning.'

Fran ignored my mumbles as she scavenged in my wallet for a tip. The restaurant was devoid of any other customers, except for a young woman, sitting close to our table, on colourful cushions. Fran noticed my quizzical look and said, 'This is Maria. We're taking her home, as the others have just left.'

I remembered her now. She'd sat quietly in the corner all evening, tucking into each plateful of dessert, and was now finishing any remaining crumbs. I was eager to make amends for ignoring her earlier and reached over to shake her hand. A yawning waitress was standing close by, to usher us to the door. As we stood to leave, I asked Maria where she was staying.

She looked a little sad, as the words tumbled out in a soft Parisian accent. 'This is my last night in Stone Town and tomorrow I will return to Paris. I am staying in a hostel–nearby I think–but in the dark, it is not so easy to find.'

The narrow streets were deserted as we ambled out of the restaurant in search of her accommodation. As Fran probed Maria for clues on its whereabouts, my thoughts returned to the worn trousers I'd given to the tailor. How could I have forgotten to collect them with an early departure planned for the morning? Although annoyed, I raised a smile and began chatting with Maria as she sauntered through the dark streets, searching for her room. An hour later, my smile had faded, and Maria was seated on a bench, asking for water. While she stared blankly at the nearby houses, I whispered to Fran. 'I'm sure we've walked down this alleyway three times already.'

Fran ignored my remark and called out to Maria. 'Does this place look familiar? Can you think of anything special about your hostel to help us find it?'

Her eyes welled. 'In the dark, it is so hard to see. But I think my hostel has a wooden door, with carvings on.'

'A wooden door,' I mumbled. 'Nearly every house in Stone Town has a carved door. It's what Zanzibar's famous for.'

Fran squeezed my arm and whispered for me to hush. She then turned to Maria and said, 'That's okay, we'll help you. Now, do you remember the name of your hostel?'

Maria was clueless. I understood why she'd been ditched at the restaurant. She'd been abandoned with the knowledge that a sleeping drunk and his compassionate wife would take her home. Together, we trudged through the town as Maria peered down each side street. It felt like *Groundhog Day* as we wandered through nameless alley-ways, ending back at the closed restaurant much later. While Maria sat on a wall, I leaned close to Fran. 'I'm not being funny, but let's just run off. She'll never catch us.'

Her eyes widened in surprise. 'I know you don't mean it.'

I couldn't help but share my frustrations again. 'She must be used to being lost all the time. I'm surprised she made it out of France on her own.'

I was tired of being the Good Samaritan, but a sense of duty pulled at my conscience as we set off for another circuit of the town. While I wallowed in self-pity, my thoughts turned to the mended trousers, sitting on a shelf, somewhere close. As Maria and Fran set off to search another backstreet, I sat on a bench to rest my eyes. I was soon brought to my senses by the sound of Fran, calling out, 'Au revoir. Good luck with your journey home.'

I looked up to see Fran waving to Maria, who'd entered the courtyard of a hostel and was now making her way to the front door. As soon as she was safely inside, Fran explained that Maria had recognised the trees in the front garden. I didn't have the heart to mention that we'd walked past the same hostel twice before. I was just glad that she was safe, and we were heading home at last.

By now, I felt I knew every building and alleyway in Stone Town and after a few more turnings, we were outside our hostel. A group of young lads stood nearby, and Fran went over to talk with them. I didn't feel quite as sociable and opted for the concrete steps instead. One boy dashed towards a nearby alleyway, but I took little notice and closed my eyes, hoping she'd soon stop chatting.

I was prodded awake soon after. This time it wasn't Fran, but an elderly man grinning at me! I recognised him at once but couldn't quite grasp the situation. It was the tailor I'd met many hours earlier, and he was carrying a parcel. While I'd been napping, Fran had persuaded one of the young lads to find his shop. Despite the late hour, he'd insisted on fulfilling his duty, donning a white gown and slippers to walk to our hostel.

I held back tears and gave him a hug, then held the trousers up to the streetlight to inspect them. They'd been diligently and professionally repaired. The tailor bid us goodnight and slipped away without another word. Fran then steered me up a flight of stairs to our bedroom, cranked the air conditioner to its maximum, and switched on the overhead fan. Despite the noise and swishing of air, I was asleep within seconds.

We woke hours later, to the sound of knocking. I opened the door to find our smiling hostel owner. 'Good morning, bwana. Your taxi is waiting, to take you to the harbour. I hope you enjoy the dawn crossing.'

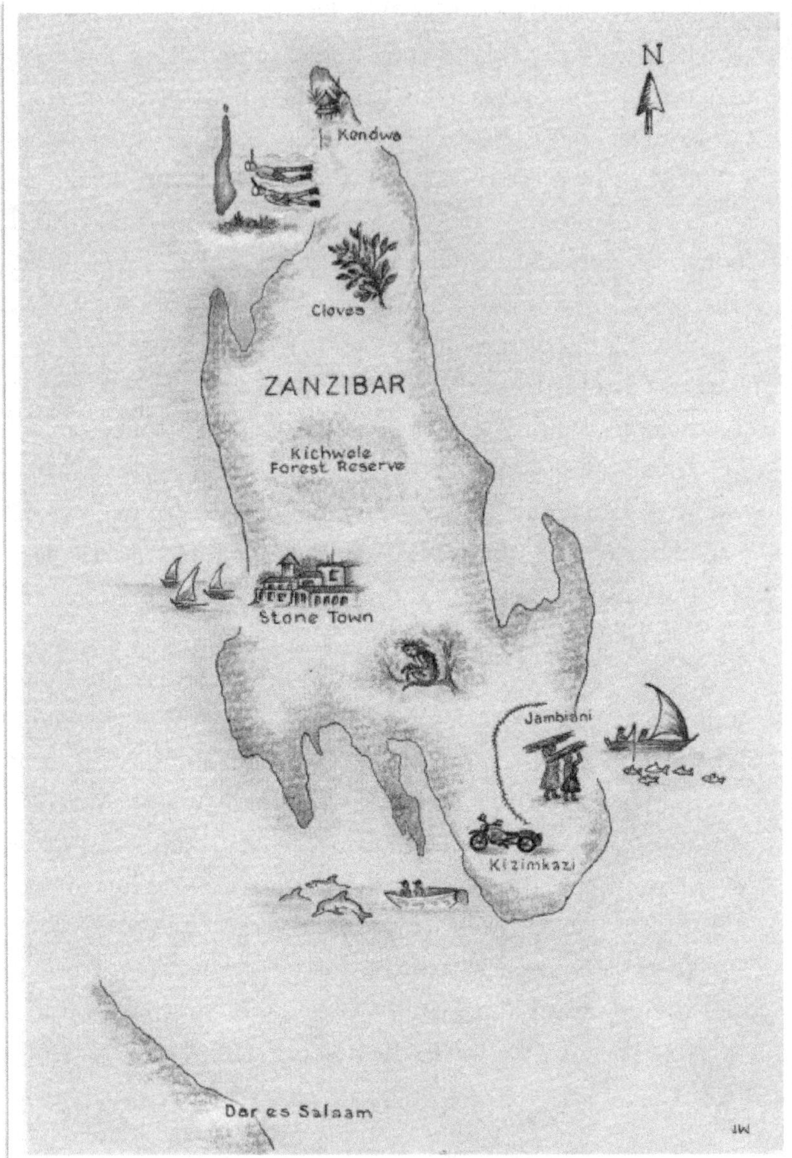
N
Kendwa
Cloves
ZANZIBAR
Kichwele
Forest Reserve
Stone Town
Jambiani
Kizimkazi
Dar es Salaam
JW

Last One Standing

"A new challenge keeps the brain kicking and the heart ticking."
E.A Bucchianeri

The ferry ploughed through the ocean towards Dar es Salaam, passing anchored dhows sitting low in the water, their lifeless sails waiting for an early breeze. Some would carry spices to the mainland, before transportation to the four corners of the globe, by cargo ship or airfreight. Despite the tranquil crossing, the late night had left us edgy, triggering a silly disagreement on a trivial matter. By the time the ferry docked, we were not on speaking terms. The argument left us ripe for exploitation by the waiting taxi drivers, who studied the disembarking passengers. Our Mexican standoff continued as we marched down the gangplank a few metres apart.

Through a gap in the crowd, a man reached out to tug at my backpack. He had cropped hair, narrow eyes, and a permanent smile. Despite the shocked expression on my face, he laughed softly and said, 'Jambo, bwana. I am your taxi driver. Please, sir, let me take your bag.'

Before I had time to argue, the rucksack was prised from my back and lifted easily onto his head. He strode quickly across the tarmac towards a row of parked cars, ignoring my cries to slow down. During the unplanned interruption, I'd lost sight of Fran and glanced around the quayside. I spotted her rucksack, on top of a shiny black head, moving away from me at a 30-degree angle. She was behind her luggage, in close pursuit.

Although I called out to her, my words were lost in the bustling crowd. I didn't want to lose sight of my luggage, but felt fearful of moving too far from Fran. I reached out to gain the attention of my uninvited porter, just as he stopped by the side of a road-weary minivan. After placing the pack inside, he turned to face me with another beaming smile. 'Good morning, mister. I am the best taxi driver in town. Where are you going today?'

Instead of answering, I looked around the crowded wharf for Fran. Initially, all I saw were black faces scurrying across the busy waterfront, but a reddened face stood out from the crowd, pinned to the inside window of a minivan, 40 metres away. She was frantically waving and calling out something, but from so far away, I had no idea what she was saying.

My driver had been joined by two helpers and they stood close by, cajoling me into the back of their vehicle. 'Please, sir, we must hurry. We are the best taxi company. Where would you like to go?'

A sudden thought came to mind, of Fran's mum at Heathrow Airport on the day of our worldwide departure. The last words she called out to me were hard to forget:

"Don't do anything silly and please look after Fran."

I needed to be with Fran and decided on a hasty exit. Just as I reached for my pack, one helper pinned it to the seat. His voice was high-pitched and tinged with anger. 'Where are you going? We are your taxi. Do not go with any others. They are bad men and will rob you.'

In one movement, I wrenched the luggage free. 'Please don't take this personally, but I've got to find my wife.'

The driver ran alongside me while I marched across the tarmac. The smiles from earlier had suddenly vanished. His voice hissed in my ear, rising in tempo with every step. 'You cannot just change your mind! I am your driver. Why are you going to another taxi company? They will rob you. Come back, please. I have the best price.'

He turned away as I reached Fran's taxi and for a moment I felt a tinge of remorse for his lost sale. Fran opened the side door and ushered me inside; both of us smiling as I reached out to squeeze her hand. I then made eye contact with the young man in the driver's seat. He'd turned to face us and was smiling brightly, along with his bald sidekick, seated in the adjacent seat. As I tried summing up the situation, the driver leaned towards us and said, 'Congratulations. You have both chosen well, as we are the number one taxi company. In my opinion, the others are all robbers. Where are you going? If you need a hotel, I know the best ones in town.'

The mention of robbers prompted me to sit upright and take a breath, before answering slowly and steadily. 'We're just after a ride to the bus station, please. How much will that be?' In response, the co-driver slid his sunglasses up, revealing bloodshot eyes. 'Relax, it will be cheap, my friend.'

As we left the waterfront, I caught sight of the earlier driver I'd abandoned. He was shaking his head while watching us pass by. The drive should have been uneventful, as it was only a quick journey. We left the harbour, joined a busy road until the first junction and then veered off towards the nearby bus station. Throughout this brief period, we were subjected to a running commentary from the driver's aide, about the high level of service they were providing. I wasn't sure what he was on about, but decided it was better to remain silent and let him continue with the sales pitch. As the minutes ticked away, he continually informed us to ignore every other taxi company, as they charged high fees and gave poor service.

Earlier in the week I'd investigated the price to pay for a taxi ride to the bus station, taking into consideration tourist rates. The advice I'd gained, led me to believe that ten US dollars would be ample. I'd prepared the money on the ferry, placing it in a handy position in my shirt pocket, rather than grappling with my hidden money belt in public. Just as we pulled into the bus station I said, 'Thanks, guys. How much do we owe you?'

'Thirty dollars, bwana,' was the monotone reply from our driver.

My heart thumped hard as I replied, 'Thirty dollars for a five-minute journey!'

As the driver turned to face me, his smile from earlier had vanished. 'Please. You owe us 30 dollars. We always give the best service.'

I shook my head and tried laughing away the matter. He was trying his luck, but I felt prepared to respond accordingly. 'Look, mate, it was a just a short journey. We were advised it would be about ten dollars. You keep saying you're the best, but what did we get for our money? Was there a tranquil drive past the President's Palace? Or a guided tour of the city, in air-conditioned comfort?'

Fran gripped my arm, but I stayed calm and pulled the note from my shirt pocket. 'Look, here's ten dollars. That's a reasonable price. You know it and so do I.'

In reply, he snapped back an answer. 'I'm not taking that. The price is 30 dollars.'

I was keen to get out of the taxi and nudged Fran into action. The driver was quick to respond and burst from his seat, before running around the front of the car. He thrust his face inches from mine and began to yell. 'You owe me 30 dollars, or I will take your luggage as payment!'

My left knee began shaking, but I met his gaze and wiped fresh spittle from my face. Ignoring the knot in my stomach, I turned to Fran. 'Grab your bag. We're getting on the bus.'

We edged around the side of the bus towards the door. Every passenger was watching from the empty window frames, their thoughts hidden behind blank expressions. One passenger was staring directly at me and as our eyes met, he momentarily held up six fingers then dropped his hands and looked away. Was he giving me a signal? As the driver and his back-up followed us to the door, I ushered Fran towards the steps and turned once more to reason with them. 'I really don't want to make a big deal out of this and appreciate the ride here. Please take your ten dollars.'

The response was another torrent of abuse. In desperation, I climbed the steps and leaned towards the driver. 'Excuse me, but we've just taken a taxi ride from the nearby harbour. What do you think we should pay?'

He revved the bus impatiently and said quietly, 'It is not my problem. All I am after is your tickets, as you are holding up the bus.'

While handing them over, I couldn't help but gripe. 'You've been so helpful. Do drop by for tea if ever you're in England.'

Rows of black faces watched silently as we looked around for vacant seats. A persistent fly took advantage of the fact that my arms were pinned down with luggage. It continually blitzed my ears as we shuffled down the stuffy aisle. I tried ignoring the buzzing and smiled at the passengers, even though we were being followed by the taxi driver and his friend.

The only available seats were in the back row. There were two, side by side, but these had become one and a half, as the next-door neighbour was a large black woman, with a frizz of dark hair. She scowled as we came closer and ignored my friendly greeting as I squeezed into position next to her. Without a word, she turned her attention to a teenager outside, who was holding up a basket, filled with an assortment of snacks.

The sour-faced woman hemmed me in to my left and the two men from our taxi blocked my view of the aisle. To my right sat Fran's rigid frame; her gaze never leaving the floor. The bus rattled into gear and left the station. At this point, I was hoping the men would accept my earlier offer. Instead, the taxi driver raised his voice so that every passenger could hear. 'You owe me 30 dollars. Give it to me now!'

The bus gathered speed on the city's outskirts, and still he ranted about the amount we owed. It was only then that the first shred of doubt crossed my mind. What if 30 dollars was correct? What did 20 dollars difference really mean to us? Fran came to the rescue. I don't know how, but she discreetly found a ten-dollar note and passed it over.

I stood up, cleared my throat, and called for attention from the onlookers. 'Good morning. I hope you've enjoyed the free sideshow this morning. As you can see, these men are not happy, as we have yet to pay the taxi bill. For those of you that are interested, I will repeat this only once. We've just been unexpectedly charged 30 dollars, for the brief journey from the harbour. Although we initially offered ten, this was clearly not enough for them. To help end the argument, I'm happy to split the difference and pay 20.'

I joined Fran's note with mine and offered them to the driver. He waved them away and leaned closer to his friend, who was busy whispering in his ear. I decided on an alternative approach and called out, 'I am now putting the money in his shirt pocket.' I reached over and slid the notes inside, hoping that he wouldn't be insulted by such an act.

Although I could feel sweat dripping down my back, I managed a brave smile and waited for a reply. I was met by silence by the driver, who turned his attention back to his friend. As they spoke in hushed tones, I decided it was time to bring the charade to an end. I raised my chin and spoke as clearly as possible, despite the palpitations in my heart. 'Thank you, ladies and gentlemen. The problem is now resolved, and the show is over. I will not be talking again until we reach Nairobi.'

I reached for a book and squeezed onto the seat, trying to ignore my trembling left knee against the fleshy thigh of my neighbour. While easing out a guarded smile, I turned to face her once more, hoping for a Good Samaritan to come to the rescue. Instead, with folded arms, she silently gazed outside at the passing buildings.

I turned my attention back to the taxi driver and noticed that even with 20 dollars in his breast pocket he refused to budge. His friend began whispering again, which produced another barrage of accusations. I sensed at that point he thought he'd found the golden goose. My shaking knee began to recover, and I eased back into the seat, ensuring my guidebook was high enough to shield my face.

Moments later, my accuser turned around and made his way to the front of the bus, calling for his friend to join him. The bus pulled over and they silently disembarked. As they walked away, I noticed a sly grin on the face of the taxi driver. Two hours later, the bus stopped at a roadside café and while queuing for a drink we met the man who'd signalled at us from the bus window. He congratulated us on keeping calm, but advised we'd paid 14 dollars too much for such a short taxi ride!

After an overnight stay in Nairobi, we boarded the morning flight to Harare, Zimbabwe. We were both a little nervous about travelling to Zimbabwe, due to the strict sanctions imposed on the country because of election rigging and human rights issues. The customs official at Harare airport did little to lift our spirits as he scrutinised our passports and enquired about our visit. I explained that we'd booked a holiday with an adventure travel company and were due to be picked up at the airport, then taken to a camping ground. He asked for proof, checked the itinerary and then waved us through without another word.

After collecting our luggage, we waited to be picked up by our guide, but no one arrived. Impatience drove me to pace the sparkling corridors, watching the cleaner with intrigue as he re-swept and re-polished the shiny tiles. I called him over for advice on the camp location and estimated taxi fare, then asked for the nearest ATM. He stared at me for a moment and then said, 'They're not used so much these days. Why do you need one?'

'To get some money for a taxi.'

'Do you have US dollars on you?' he asked.

I nodded once and he continued to speak. 'Our currency is in freefall, and the ATM will probably be empty. Stick with US dollars if you can.'

He then returned to his cleaning duties, as we strolled outside into bright sunshine to begin the next part of our journey. During our transit in a spotless taxi, we tried chatting with the well-groomed driver, but he seemed more interested in the news on the radio. When he finally spoke, it was about greed, corruption and the spiralling economy. I gave up talking with him and turned my thoughts to those we were about to meet. While we'd been preoccupied with Kilimanjaro and Zanzibar, they'd travelled south for many weeks, sometimes on the road for long hours, as they roamed between game reserves, tribal villages and coastal settlements.

We arrived at the campsite a few hours before the truck, which gave us time to meet with the owner. He was in his mid-thirties, wide shouldered and clean shaven, with long blonde hair, styled into a ponytail. Despite his easy manner, he soon shared that the economic situation was hurting his business. Even with bright sunshine, an inviting pool, a well-stocked bar, warm showers and cooking facilities, there was still a distinct lack of guests. Some travel companies were staying away from Zimbabwe, causing a ripple effect across the tourism sector.

By their very nature, overland trucking adventures can be risky at times. These risks are constantly being managed and in rare situations, schedules can change at the last minute. This is mainly due to natural disasters, severe illness with a passenger or crewmember, or political instability. At the most extreme, it's because of acts of terrorism or war.

We took up the invite to take a tour of the ancient rock art found on the edges of the camp. The paintings, still in pristine condition, depicted hunters and beasts now lost to a modern world and urbanisation.

Late in the afternoon, a dusty yellow truck rolled into camp and stopped alongside the reception area. One by one, the passengers emerged from the doorway, their eyes glazed, and their movements sluggish. Some jumped onto the grass, calling out to their friends to meet them in the bar, while others clambered down the steps, complaining about cramped muscles.

I thought back to our time in Nairobi, when we'd briefly met some of them by the hotel pool. Back then, they'd mostly been strangers to each other, exchanging names, places of birth and job titles. A day later, they'd set off on their adventure, across Kenya and Tanzania, including overnight camps in the Serengeti, before spending time in Malawi. After such a diverse journey, it was hardly surprising that none of them seemed to recognise us.

We stood nearby, watching as they came to life after being confined during the long drive. They mostly ranged in age from their early twenties to late thirties, with an even mix of genders. The first voice I heard sounded like a Londoner, followed by the chirpy tone of a larrikin Australian. One by one they walked away, clutching daypacks and empty water bottles, their sights set firmly on the bar.

As we were the first new passengers since Nairobi, I'd been hoping for at least one friendly smile, but as the last passenger wandered past, I shrugged my shoulders and turned to face Fran. She squeezed my hand, somehow reading my mind. 'Ali, I'm sure they're a friendly bunch. They just look a bit exhausted, that's all.'

'I guess you're right. Maybe we'll also look that way when we arrive in Cape Town.'

Then I had a sudden thought and asked, 'Do you remember when we turned up at the conservation project in Ecuador?'

'Yes, of course, but what are you getting at?'

'Well, it was after sunset, and no one looked up as we entered the jungle camp. They were more interested in their evening meal than the two red-faced strangers trying to fight off the bugs and insects. Don't you see? It's a similar scenario. Just like in the Amazon, we're the newcomers again.'

Fran wouldn't get drawn into a debate about the apparent unfriendliness of the passengers. Instead, she laid down a simple challenge. 'Come on, we can stand out here on our own and look even more out of place, or go inside and start to mingle. The quicker they get to know us, the better.'

Partway through our first beer, I got chatting to Chris, a sunburnt accountant who'd taken an extended holiday from the northern suburbs of London, to enjoy an African adventure. He spoke quickly, the pitch of his voice changing as he shared snippets of their time in the game reserves. He described close encounters with a bull elephant, drunken nights under the stars, and lions making a kill.

Then he dropped his voice a little and said, 'The wildlife's been amazing, but today was a long day on the road. We've been hanging out for a cold beer for hours. I'm glad that tomorrow is a free day. Mind you, camping by Lake Malawi was out of this world! I'm too tired to tell you about it now but remind me later. By the way, if you're interested you can share my job while we're on the road.'

Intrigued, I asked, 'What does it involve?'

'Oh, it's easy. I've been sitting in the same seat since Nairobi, right next to the door. Whenever someone wants a toilet break, they let me know and I push the buzzer by my side, to inform Tony.'

'Who's Tony?' I asked.

'The driver, of course. He's English as well. With you two on board, that makes six Brits altogether. The other passengers are from Australia and New Zealand, with a few German and Dutch to add to the mix.'

A girl called his name, prompting a hasty departure and the promise to talk again later. I caught sight of another man entering the room and watched as he collected a beer, exchanged a few high fives and made his way across the floor. His eyes locked onto mine and he smiled widely while striding towards us.

He was about 30, similar in height to me, with short dark hair and tanned skin. He held out a hand and said, 'Hi guys. My name's Jeff and I'm the guide for the trip to Cape Town. It has been a long day on the road, so we're all feeling the strain.'

He studied the piece of paper in his hand and said, 'You two must be Alistair and Francine.'

Our smiles confirmed the answer, which led him to call out for silence. The room hushed momentarily, as all eyes turned our way. 'Guys, dinner will be served soon. I've arranged a barbeque by the campfire. I'm sure you've all noticed the two new passengers. This is Alistair and Francine. It looks like we have two more Brits on the tour, which should even up the banter a little!'

A ripple of laughter filled the room and I noticed Chris standing in the corner, smiling widely. Jeff then said, 'You'll be glad to know that tomorrow is a free day. You can relax by the pool, take a walk to enjoy the rock art, or stay at camp and get your washing done. For those who fancy a game of golf, the truck can drop you off in the morning on the way to town for provisions.'

After the brief speech, he turned his attention to Fran and me. Without prompting, he apologised for the lack of airport pickup and insisted on paying the taxi fee. Then he called out to the barman for two beers and handed us one each. Before we had the chance to return the favour, he headed towards the kitchen to help speed up the evening meal.

Armed with fresh US dollars and a new sense of vigour, we went in search of Chris. He introduced us to those around him, but like every other passenger their thoughts were on hot food and a few drinks, not the two recent additions.

The early night seemed to reinvigorate most passengers and during breakfast, we exchanged more than just names. Chris asked if we wanted to join him and a few others for golf. Fran declined, as she'd volunteered to assist with preparing dinner, but with little else on offer I decided to tag along.

The truck dropped us off by the golf course entrance, alongside a solitary car, parked outside. Even though we failed to meet the dress code standards, the man behind the desk ignored our round-necked T-shirts, shorts, and trainers, and greeted us with a friendly smile. An optional extra, which we snapped up, was the chance for each of us to hire a caddy. I got introduced to Edmund, a skinny black teenager with a goofy grin. He wore an Adidas Polo shirt, chinos and the kind of golfing shoes I expected to see worn by a professional.

Just to make matters clear, I'm not a golfer. I've played countless times, mainly in England, with friends and family. By nine holes, my concentration usually wavers. I then try to speed up the game by taking risky shots, far beyond my capacity. This leads to frustration, lost balls, even riskier shots and many lost matches. A few rounds per year are usually enough for me.

As we strolled outside with our golf trolleys, I expected to see unkempt fairways scorched from the sun due to the water restrictions. Instead, we came across a lush, undulating course, with manicured fairways, flanked by majestic trees. The 18th green was nearby, protected by a deep bunker, its velvety lawn awaiting the first ball of the day.

I joined a four ball and shook hands with Terrence and Jez, two friends from New Zealand who were also on the truck. Quiet and unassuming, they peeled away to study the match card. After a series of practice swings, they both delivered perfect drives, while Chris stood close to me and whispered about the journey so far. 'Overland trips are not for everyone. You need to pace yourself, I reckon. In Malawi, we visited heaps of markets and bartered for all types of handmade souvenirs. The hold of the truck is filled with bongo drums, spears and carved giraffes. My rucksack is bursting and I won't be buying anything else on this trip.'

'What about the game parks you've seen so far?' I asked.

He placed his ball onto the tee, took a practise swing and called out, 'I'll never forget the Serengeti, for as long as I live.'

He sliced the ball towards nearby trees and waved me forward for my turn. As I searched for a suitable club, Edmund warned me about the slope of the fairway and pointed out a faraway bunker. He continued to advise me throughout the next few holes, despite the scorecard racking up quickly. Halfway through the fifth, I studied the flag from afar and asked Edmund to take the shot for me. He smiled widely, then selected a five iron and delivered a perfect shot onto the green, followed up by a birdie putt.

While I warmed up for the next hole, he attempted to address my swing, but I challenged him to the longest drive instead. After pocketing the win, he opened up a little about the sanctions, and shared that one day he planned to become a professional. For now, his main income came from caddying visitors, which were few and far between.

I decided to give up after the ninth hole, which prompted Chris to do the same. Maybe it was the heat, the humidity or the fact that compared to our caddies, we were an embarrassment. I handed my clubs to Edmund, along with some American dollars, and wished him all the best.

During the walk back to camp, we found ourselves beside people carrying empty fuel cans. We didn't ask and they didn't tell. Compared to the bright and breezy faces of those I'd seen in Zanzibar, these Africans rarely made eye contact, as they strode quietly along the side of the road. Others carried baskets of food on their heads, but very few carried smiles.

The following morning, a chilly wind and overcast sky hastened our exit from the camp. After breakfast, the tents and backpacks were bundled into the hold, in readiness for a swift departure. I climbed on board with Fran, both of us excited and a little nervous as we contemplated our first day on the road. The seats were set out in long rows, underneath the side windows and it soon became clear that established passengers were moving to their favourite spots.

We stood awkwardly in the aisle while they shuffled past and settled into their preferred seats. A few minutes later, the vacant spots were visible, including two near the back that caught our eye. Fran made her way towards them, chatting to those around her as she did so. I threw my hat onto the nearest seat of the two, then reached out to close the door. As I did so, a friendly voice called out, 'Leave it please, mate, there's a few more to come.'

Moments later, two men arrived, hurling banter at each other as they headed for their seats, which happened to be the ones we were now in. They stood in the aisle, giggling for a few seconds before turning their attention to us. The nearest was a thickset man with wispy brown hair, on the verge of thinning. He was in his late twenties, dressed in camouflage shorts and a faded T-shirt. Unshaven and red eyed, he stared down at me. 'Hey, mate, get off the chair. That's my seat.'

Outwardly I smiled, but my heart sank at such rudeness. This wasn't how overland passengers were meant to act. Then I noticed that all the other passengers were watching. Was this some type of initiation test? I laughed off the incident and held out my hand. 'Hi, I'm Ali and this is my wife, Fran. I didn't quite catch your name.'

His hands remained locked to his side. 'My name's Troy and that's my seat. I've been in it since we left Nairobi.'

I retracted my hand as the first threads of doubt crossed my mind. This would be a long journey if most passengers acted like Troy. I turned my attention to his friend, who was a few inches taller than Troy, with a wild thatch of red hair, green eyes, and broad shoulders. He held out his hand and grasped mine, then turned to smile at Fran. 'Welcome aboard, guys. The name's Ryan, and don't mind Troy. He's always grumpy.'

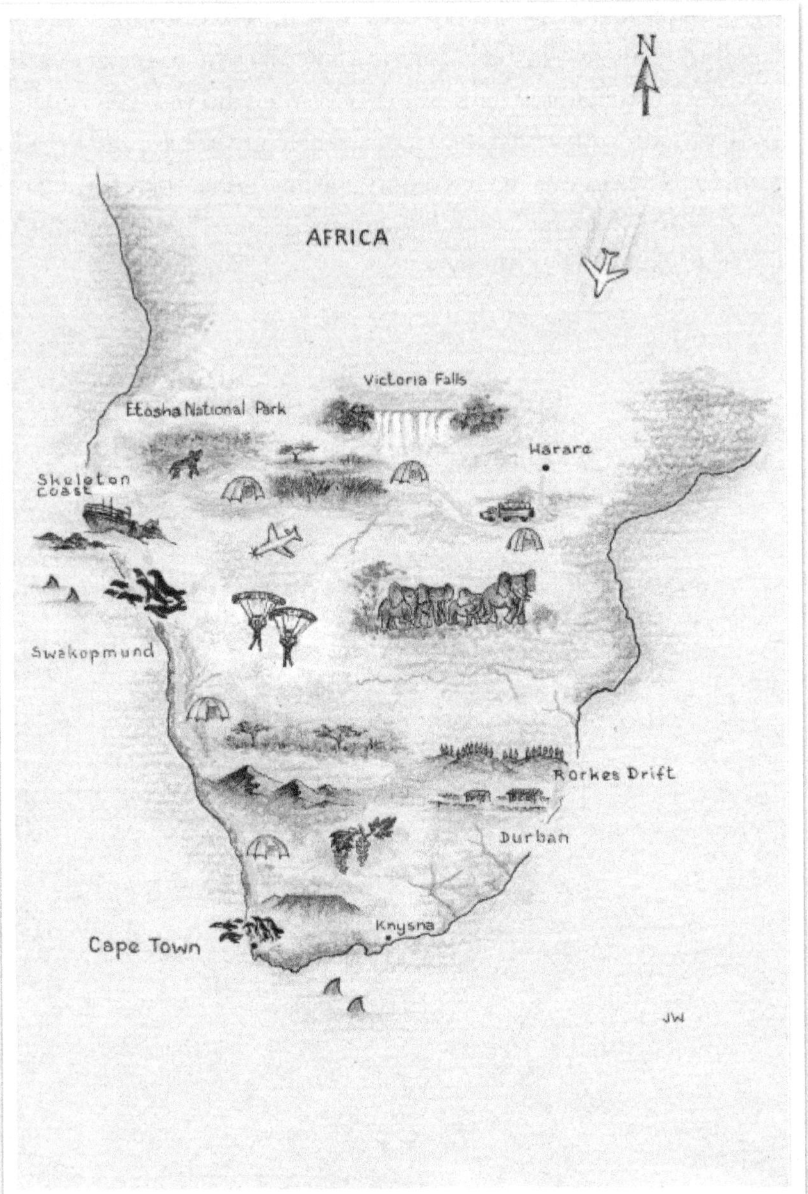
N
AFRICA
Victoria Falls
Etosha National Park
Harare
Skeleton Coast
Swakopmund
Rorkes Drift
Durban
Knysna
Cape Town
JW

Driver's Seat

If you want to go fast, go alone
If you want to go far, go together
African Proverb

Zimbabwe has sixteen official languages, but the most widely used are English, Shona, and Ndebele. The Shona are the largest ethnic group in the country, numbering close to nine million people. Zimbabwe gets its name from two Shona words: *mba,* which means house, and *bwe*, which means stone. Put them together and you have the *House of Stone*. The stone houses refer to what was once a great city, covering 80 hectares, located in the southern half of the country, 320 kilometres from the capital city of Harare.

Although now abandoned, the city once flourished as part of a great trading empire, with a population of 10,000. With fertile lands and rich mineral deposits nearby, the city grew to become the largest settlement in southern Africa. All this occurred between the 11th and 15th centuries and sometime after that it began to falter, before falling into ruin. No one is certain of the reasons for its demise, with experts divided on whether it was through war, crop failure, mineral depletion, or overexpansion. The remains are now known as the Great Zimbabwean Ruins and are recognised as a World Heritage Site by UNESCO.

The drive to the ruins took about four hours. During this period, I caught sight of Troy, sleeping soundly, mouth wide open and legs sprawled across the aisle. Fran began chatting to the nearest passengers and we soon discovered that most on board had grown used to Troy and his brash behaviour. Most, it seemed, gave him a wide berth, or saw his outbursts as nothing more than childish rants. Ironically, everyone seemed to like his friend, Ryan.

There were no glass windows on the sides of the truck. Instead, we had transparent plastic sheeting, robust enough to deflect a chilly wind, flexible enough to roll up, and designed to be tied down firmly whenever we parked in towns or cities. As the sun found its strength, the sides were hauled high, allowing a welcome breeze to circulate throughout the cabin.

It was just after midday when we stepped off the truck, each of us bathed in sweat, and seeking shelter from the sun, rather than listening to the welcome speech by the enthusiastic guide. Our first stop was the Great Enclosure, home to a conical tower, nine metres high and constructed from granite. While flanked by high walls, the guide called us together to share a few facts about the abandoned city. We soon learned that most buildings had been constructed without the use of mortar between each rectangular block of stone.

A few hardy trees grew close to the main wall, offering much-needed shade, but before too long we headed towards a boulder-strewn hill. With far-reaching views of a shimmering valley, I should have felt more inspired, but with each step the pounding in my head increased. Despite the sun's glare, I did my best to listen intently to the guide, especially when told about the eight carved birds that were once known to have decorated the walls and columns of the city. Standing over four feet tall, each bird was carved from soapstone and have since become the national symbol of Zimbabwe. Their image is found on the national flag, coins and banknotes, as well as many government buildings.

In 1889, a European hunter by the name of Willi Posselt is known to have visited the site, when it was still relatively untouched. During his stay, he hacked one of the birds from its plinth and is said to have paid off the local tribes with blankets to keep them happy. The stolen bird eventually got sold to Cecil Rhodes, the man who founded De Beers Diamond Company and was once Prime Minister of the Cape Colony.

A year later, most of the remaining birds were removed by a British archaeologist called James Theodore Bent, to be housed in the South African museum in Cape Town. A portion of one bird ended up in Germany. It wasn't until Zimbabwe declared independence in 1980 that the task of repatriation began. To date, seven soapstone birds have been returned, but the one sold to Rhodes remains in Cape Town. It's on display to those lucky enough to get invited into Groote Schuur, his former estate, which he bequeathed to the nation.

After hearing about the birds, I decided to head back to the truck for water. My only thought was to find somewhere cool, but I soon found myself surrounded by two high walls, running in parallel. The air between them was hot and still, but this didn't seem to bother the handful of visitors trying to take creative photos of the granite stone. I dashed past them and set my sights on the truck.

After a quick scout, I soon discovered that the doors were locked and the sides had been tied down. Instead of returning to the ruins, I sat under the shade of a tree and rested my back against its narrow trunk. It didn't take long before I had company. There were about seven of them, some male, others female, all of them black, and most of them younger than me.

They stood nearby, calling out for attention while holding up a selection of carvings and trinkets, including colourful murals, as tall as a man. With months of travel ahead of me, I felt reluctant to purchase anything on a whim and called out, 'No thanks. I'm not feeling the best. The only thing I'm after right now is a drink of water.'

The nearest man studied me closely and said, 'Mister, I have water from my village, which you can have for free. But somehow, I don't think it will be good for you.'

He then took another step closer and said, 'Have you seen our carvings? They have been crafted in the local village, but we don't get many visitors these days. We need to sell them to help feed our families.'

The appeals were hard to ignore, and I stood up before taking hold of one of the carvings. This prompted the others to step closer, and within seconds, they all surrounded me. Just then, I heard my name being called. It was Chris, strolling towards the truck, followed closely by our driver and the other passengers. He was holding aloft an ice-cold bottle of mineral water and called out, 'Alistair, we're about to board. Fran's been looking for you in the café!'

Most sellers turned half circle and headed towards the returning passengers, allowing me time to steal on board and search for my water bottle. As the engine kicked into life, the plastic strips were hauled high, revealing the faces of the sellers below, still waiting for their first sale. Those that had travelled through Malawi had been through this scenario dozens of times, and judging by their body language, were no longer interested in bartering for hand crafted souvenirs. Some were already listening to music through earphones, or glugging water, while awaiting our departure.

On impulse, I leaned over the side of the truck and called out to the man I'd spoken with earlier. He stepped closer and fanned a large mural, revealing a series of abstract sketches, framed by an ochre-coloured border. One segment resembled a soapstone bird, and I thought back to the guide, talking passionately about the importance of the figurine to the people of Zimbabwe.

Over the noise of the engine, the man named his price. I heard Chris call out to me about the importance of bartering, but Tony had just beeped the horn, signalling an imminent departure. A teenage girl then held out two clay masks, cradled in the palms of her hands. She called out a hopeful price but lowered it when I shook my head. I accepted her next offer, which produced a bright smile as I handed over some notes, scooped up the masks and turned my attention to the man with the mural.

As the wheels began to turn, I negotiated a last-second deal as the man jogged alongside the truck. He got his sale, and I got my mural. After waving goodbye, I returned to my seat, the proud owner of two carvings and a colourful piece of cloth, large enough to fill the side compartment of my rucksack! As we drove away, I studied the mementos, while Fran sat beside me, shaking her head and smiling softly. For sure, they'd been purchased hastily, but hopefully the sale had helped the vendors a little.

It must be hard to gain a sale from those that have already travelled across East Africa, especially when economic sanctions or political unrest, ward off many other travellers. It suddenly struck me that as tourists we were protected from the harsh realities of real life, hurtling past abandoned vehicles, while Bob Marley wailed in stereo from the truck cabin.

Our next destination was Gweru, home to Antelope Park, a long-established stopover for those on overland trucks. Set in over 3,000 acres of open savannah, the park offers visitors the chance to experience wildlife and outdoor pursuits, without having to give up on creature comforts. It's not only adventure tourists that spend time at Gweru. Honeymooners and weekenders are drawn to the private lodges, while those seeking a wilder setting can opt for safari style tents, located close to the river's edge. There is even the option to have curious giraffes on your guest list, with various wedding packages on offer to suit budget and taste.

Although the park is home to many species, including zebra, giraffe, warthog and gazelle, there are few predators and no wild elephants or rhinos. Jeff explained that the park catered to those in search of a taste of the African wilderness, with the chance to get up close and personal to domesticated elephants and juvenile lions.

Like many elephants around the world that are born in captivity or orphaned, the ones at Antelope Park paid their way, mainly by ferrying tourists on guided walks into the surrounding grassland. The lions in the park were not free roaming. They'd either been raised as cubs or been taken into custody after being displaced or orphaned. Most, it seemed, were juveniles and it was these that were used for the *Walking with Lions* experience.

Although the chance to walk with lions caused a stir of excitement within the group, I felt apprehensive about signing up. Fran had similar feelings too, with niggling doubts that the lions were being exploited, so that we could enjoy a once in a lifetime experience. To ease our worries, we sought out one of the rangers and enquired further.

Johan was in his late twenties, with broad shoulders and short blonde hair. Over a coffee, he briefly explained how Antelope Park is involved in the *Lion Rehabilitation and Release into the Wild* program. This is run in conjunction with an organisation called ALERT (African Lion and Environmental Research Trust) who manage the *Walking with Lions* program at Gweru. Johan talked passionately about the lions and his hopes for their future. He also explained about habitat loss, and the depletion of prey that affects the lions in the wild today.

He then handed me a flyer with information about ALERT and their vision. It read: *To ensure viable populations of African lions are maintained, as an integral part of functional ecosystems.*

As I finished the drink, Johan said, 'Just to be clear, the lions you walk with tomorrow will never be returned to the wild, as they have become reliant on humans. Rehabilitation into the wild is just too risky. Not only for the lions, but also for anybody that may encounter them in the future. They cannot be tamed, but will never be truly wild.'

'So, what's the answer, then?' I asked.

'It's the next generation of lions, the ones that will be born in protected areas and raised by the pride, without human contact. With careful planning and lots of hard work, they can hopefully be released into the wild when ready.'

I thanked Johan and made my way to the reception building, to enquire about a booking. The staff member was busy on the phone and gestured for me to wait in the adjacent garden. Moments after walking outside I spotted movement. I dropped to my knees and held my hands out wide, to welcome the three lion cubs that came running towards me. Within seconds I was flat on my back, laughing and giggling as they bounded across my body, tumbled onto the grass and tried nipping my toes! They were the size of puppy dogs, with dark eyes and soft brown fur. Just as one of them made a beeline for my hat, the door to the reception area opened. I looked up from the grass into the shocked eyes of the receptionist, who stood with hands on hips, smiling at me from the doorway. 'How did they get here?' she asked.

I had no idea, but as we chased the cubs around the garden and called for help from the warden, I couldn't help feeling that I was in some type of dream. The good fortune continued, as I made my way towards the campsite and came across a fenced enclosure. It was home to two juvenile elephants, being fed and watered. The keeper noticed me standing nearby and gestured me forward to help. She handed me a brush, turned on a hosepipe, and asked me to scrub the nearest elephant. Mine was a young male and as I soaked his back with water, I began thinking about all the other elephants in the park. Were they all orphaned, or had some been raised in captivity? What did the future hold for them? I should have asked the girl, but she was knee deep in straw while trying to ignore the flies at her face.

My elephant seemed happy enough, munching on straw and twitching his large ears. The pungent smell of fresh dung filled my nostrils as I rubbed my hands across his grey, mottled skin. While washing under his neck, I began to chat away to my newfound friend. Maybe it was my imagination, but his ears seemed to flap slightly, as if listening to my every word. Before leaving, I gave him a hug, spreading my arms wide and listening to gurgles deep within his stomach.

Later that day, I headed to the paddock with Fran, to watch the elephants take visitors on a sunset tour. As we stepped back to allow them to pass, my elephant glanced over and playfully prodded me in the stomach with his trunk. He left a moist imprint on my T-shirt, then turned and headed towards the setting sun.

As the stars emerged, I took a walk around the campsite to gather my thoughts. The days were passing quickly, and I still had so much to learn about Africa. I was having second thoughts about the decision to sign up for the walk with lions. The painful experience with the dolphins at Zanzibar had left their mark, regarding the subject of ecotourism and the potential for unethical behaviour by tourists and travel organisations.

Releasing lions back into the wild is a vision I share. But it is a complex problem, made worse by the continual erosion of habitat and a growing population of humans. On the surface, ecotourism sounds ethical, but dig below the surface and it gets complicated. We put our trust in organisations like ALERT, hoping they are doing the right thing.

According to the National Geographic, lion populations have declined by 90% in the last 75 years. To put this in numbers, in the 1960s there were said to be 100,000 lions in the wild. That figure could now be as low as 20,000 and the numbers continue to fall.

I needed to ease my conscience and that night, while at the bar, spoke to the ranger again. As if to clear up any last doubts, he shared that the park had secured a large pocket of suitable land. All they needed was the funding to complete the purchase. Just before leaving, he placed his empty beer bottle on the table and said, 'I think

Nelson Mandela summed it up when he said, "Ultimately, conservation is about people."'

The next morning, we wrapped up and made our way towards the lions' den for a dawn walk. The main guide was waiting patiently and took the time to shake our hands. He wore a flannel shirt, khaki trousers and leather boots, which he stamped on the ground, as if to ward away the early morning chill.

He carried a walking pole, made from hardwood, which he tapped on the grass while calling for silence. 'Welcome everyone. I'm sure this is a special moment for you. But be careful. Yesterday, these lions made their first kill, and I sense a change in them. I have a few rules that I'd like you to follow. First of all, do not wander into the bush alone. Remember also, to never run from a lion or turn your back on them. Most importantly, stay close to me or the assistant guide at all times.'

A fine trail of pinkish clouds added a touch of colour to the waking sky as we set off with eight other tourists and five juvenile lions. Unlike the cubs I'd met the previous day, these were close to adulthood and far larger. They initially stayed close to the guides, but as we ventured from the compound, their confidence returned and they headed into the surrounding bush, in search of game. With no role models to hone their natural instincts, the result was a strangely humorous, yet slightly sad, experience. They blundered after skittish antelope, with little chance of pinning any down.

One female peeled away from the pack, to investigate the noise from a bubbling stream. The sight of her by the water's edge created a perfect setting for a photo. Without thought, I stole away from the group, ducked under a branch, and moved closer to capture the moment. As I crouched low for a better angle, the deep voice of our guide boomed across the open space. 'Bwana, beware! Look behind you.'

My stomach knotted as I stood upright, hoping it wasn't me that the guide was shouting at. A glance towards the distant scrub revealed all. Lying flat in the red dirt was a juvenile lioness, studying me with interest. Even from 40 metres away I could see her sharp green eyes, locked onto mine. I spun around and spotted the guide, about the same distance away, in the opposite direction. Fran was standing close to him, her hands covering her mouth.

For a few seconds, my world stood still. Nothing moved. The lioness stared at me, the guide called out to the animal and Fran remained by his side, stunned into silence. My heart pounded furiously, but I remembered the earlier advice and willed my legs to stay rooted to the spot. The guide made the first move and ran towards me, waving his walking pole and shouting for the lioness to move away. It ignored the distraction and continued to stare across the grass, where I stood motionless.

Then suddenly, the lioness charged. For a split second, I stared into wild green eyes as she sprung from the dirt and quickly gained momentum. Some primal instinct told me to run. My boots dug into the mud as I sprinted towards the guide. Fran began yelling, but her frantic calls were drowned out by the fearful thoughts in my head:

I'm being chased by a lion!

Before reaching the guide, I sensed imminent danger. I stopped in my tracks and turned to face the lioness. I stood tall and braced my legs as she approached, still running at speed, but poised as if ready to pounce. The guide arrived a fraction before the lioness, thrusting his walking pole into the air while calling out. She changed direction at the last second and skimmed past, her tail swishing against my legs. As the animal raced away, Fran ran towards me, her face flushed with anger and relief. 'What the hell were you doing? Didn't you listen to the guide?'

'I was just trying to get a decent photo.' I eased out a smile, but already felt foolish while trying to explain.

The guide appeared at my side, panting while shaking his head. He spoke slowly and firmly, his eyes never leaving mine. 'Mister, you are a crazy fool. Why did you do that? Please stay close to me from now on!'

During the remainder of the excursion, I rarely left his side. Instead of looking for photo opportunities, I chatted to him about the walking with lions program and the challenges ahead. As we traipsed back to camp, weary but happy, I shook his hand and apologised once more. He smiled gently and said, 'Although you acted foolishly today, I think you learned a valuable lesson about the African bush. Please remember that the animals can be unpredictable and dangerous, no matter how friendly they look. Best of luck with your travels.'

On our last morning, we discovered a large compound, which was home to older lions. They'd grown too big to use in the *Walking with Lions* program and now looked to be without a home. I had no idea what the future held for them but felt a tinge of sadness as they paced the secure area. A niggling doubt crept over me as we drove towards Bulawayo. Would the lioness that chased me ever get the chance to raise cubs? If so, would they ever taste freedom and get the chance to live in the wild?

Some passengers on our truck also looked like they'd been cooped up for too long. A few had given up full-time jobs for the chance of a worldwide trip. One passenger was partway through a university degree and the rest were just happy to escape monotony for a while. Either way, they were in Africa to have the time of their lives.

The happiest passenger was a short, stocky guy, with the unusual nickname of *Horse*. Always smiling and full of laughter, Horse had only one mission: to get drunk every evening, from Nairobi to Cape Town. By all accounts, he was on target. Without exception, he'd be the last to leave the bar each evening and the final one to board the following morning. Most passengers were prepared for long days on the road, with books, water, snacks and portable music players, stashed carefully in daypacks. Each morning, Horse would roll into the truck bleary-eyed, then burp and look for a space on the floor. He'd then sleep in his ragged sleeping bag until lunchtime, then wake with a smile and ask for water.

Overland travel gets you into a rhythm. Long trips mean early morning chats, lots of reading, card games, sleeping, and plenty of time to think. Some passengers relaxed by playing music through earphones or taking photos of the passing landscape. As for Troy, he seemed to scowl too much. How could I make him happy? One thing I craved was more time to explore, but with long distances to travel this was not always possible.

We all needed space, and just outside the truck, there was more than enough. Toilet breaks were a welcome chance to get outside and stretch. The girls would head to one side of the truck to look for a log or bush to hide behind, while the boys would saunter to the nearest wheel. During one stop, I began chatting with our driver, Tony. He listened for a while as I explained about the long day on the road. In response, he said, 'I don't know why you guys sit in the back all day.'

My eyes widened. 'What do you mean? Where else can we go?'

Tony grinned and pointed to the front passenger door. 'In with me, of course. I've got three seats, air-conditioning and the best view in Africa.'

'But Jeff is up front and so is your missus.' (Tony had married the assistant guide.)

'Alistair, never forget, this is your trip. They can have a stint in the back for a change.'

All afternoon I sat shotgun, then changed over with Fran at the next toilet break. After dinner that evening, I was approached by Troy, the man whose seat I'd innocently chosen during my first morning on the truck. 'Hey, Alistair. Why aren't you sitting in the back with us?'

'I found a spare seat at the front, alongside Tony. Why don't you try it sometime?'

Thirty-two days after starting out in Nairobi, Troy finally enjoyed a bird's-eye view of the open road, while seated up front with Tony.

One of the animals we encountered

Waves of Fear

"The first river you paddle runs through the rest of your life."
Lynn Noel

By the next morning, we were heading towards Matobo Hills, declared a UNESCO World Heritage Site, because of its ecological and historical significance. Blood-red granite boulders known as *koppies* lay scattered across the parched landscape, giving shelter to elusive game. Ancient rock art is found in the wooded reserve, depicting a time when the San people lived and hunted in the surrounding hills and valleys. The San people no longer inhabit these parts, and some animal species are becoming rare, but all is not lost. Matobo Hills may be small compared to the vast East African reserves, but is vitally important in protecting rhino populations.

There are no elephants or lions in the reserve, but the exposed granite formations provide a perfect habitat for leopards. The absence of lions meant walking safaris were permitted. Surprisingly, only a handful from our truck signed up for the trip. Horse came along, which was unexpected as he usually went in search of the campsite bar. As we headed into the reserve, I noticed his worn flip-flops on the stony ground. His calloused feet were as hardened as his liver and skipped easily over the thorns and searing rocks.

Our guide was Tim, a retired soldier who stood to attention and greeted us all with a warm smile. He was tall, with a straight back, piercing blue eyes and an impressive crop of mousey hair. After a prompt from Horse, he told a few stories concerning the dark days of the bloody civil war, which eventually led to the renaming of the country, from Rhodesia to Zimbabwe. Now his motive was to help protect the rhinos, which had been forced into the reserve by a loss of habitat and poaching.

Our first sighting was from a distance. The rhino was so far away that most in the group were convinced it was a large, grey rock. Tim urged us to be patient, and after a few minutes we watched as it moved a few steps before coming to a rest. Then, once again, it resembled a large, grey rock. We were keen to get nearer, which led Tim to explain the importance of wind direction when tracking game. He also asked us to hush, as any noise would carry far.

Seemingly happy that we were committed to the cause, he demonstrated a few simple hand gestures to help with communication. We then set off in single file, with Tim at the front, leading us in a wide semi-circle along a maze of game tracks. As the sun blazed overhead, we were joined by a black cloud of flies, which continually buzzed around our exposed faces. By now, my tongue was coated in a layer of dust, kicked up by those around me.

Compared to the San people that would have used their skills and stealth to quietly approach any prey, we were a pitiful sight. Some complained of a lack of water, others stopped to remove stones from boots, and one or two asked if we could head back to the truck. In all the commotion, Tim continually asked for quiet and kept pointing ahead, but very few of us could see anything except flies and bushes.

As I reached for a last dribble of water, Tim dropped to his knees and rested an index finger vertically against his mouth. The only sound was the hum of buzzing flies near my face. I fought the urge to swish them away and crouched low, my eyes on Tim. He reached out and lightly touched my arm, then slowly pointed towards a scattering of bushes, a few metres ahead.

While shielding my eyes from the sun, I studied the terrain and in that moment my heart began racing! Close by, was an adult black rhino, grazing on a patch of grass. The only barrier between us and the two-tonne beast was a few withered trees, waiting for the rains. I looked around for Fran, who was further back with the rest of the group.

The colour had drained from her cheeks, and she was waving for me to join her. A deep grunt sounded from behind the bushes, and I returned my attention to the rhino. The flies seemed to have vanished and I could make out its wide mouth, ripping long grass from the earth. My gaze then fell upon its priceless horn, darkened with age at the tip.

A sudden breeze stirred the branches of the nearest trees and nudged our scent towards the rhino. It lifted its majestic head and grunted again, sounding like an old man mumbling in his sleep. Suddenly, all was quiet. I stood completely still, unsure whether to watch Tim for hand signals or to concentrate on the rhino. It was no longer grazing and had moved a few paces. My next thought was how to quickly get a memorable photograph, as the rhino seemed to be growing restless.

While adjusting my wide-angled lens, I heard the crack of timber, followed immediately by the sound of Tim, yelling at me to run. I peered up from the camera to see the rhino charging through the bush. I spun away, in a desperate attempt to escape from danger. In that moment, two thoughts flashed through my mind. Why was I the closest to the rhino out of our group and why hadn't I seen the fallen tree, directly behind me?

The log tripped me, and I spiralled into the red dirt, sending the camera spinning into the air as the rhino tore through the hedge. Ignoring the camera, my feet scrambled for traction as I sprinted after Tim. By the time I caught up with him, he was alongside the panic-stricken group, urging them to stop. 'It's okay,' he called. 'It was just a mock charge.'

To emphasise the point, he stopped in his tracks and pointed towards the rhino. It was still in no-man's-land but had come to a stop.

While we watched from afar, it seemed to snuffle the ground, then backed away and returned to its previous location.

We tentatively approached a second time, and the rhino seemed to settle. I found my camera, dusted it down and grabbed the chance to get a few snaps. By now, we'd learned to be whisper quiet, but the blazing sun, a rising thirst and insistent flies soon took their toll. We left the rhino in peace and headed back to camp for one more night. Within days, we were going to get soaking wet!

Known locally as Mosi-oa-Tunya, 'the smoke that thunders', Victoria Falls is renowned as one of the most spectacular waterfalls in the world. The township that has built up alongside the falls is considered by many, to be the adventure capital of Africa.

One of the most popular activities for thrill seekers involves bungee jumping from Victoria Falls Bridge, which spans the Zambezi and connects Zimbabwe with the town of Livingstone, in Zambia. Before leaping from a designated ledge, each participant gets the chance to wave at a video camera while enjoying a bird's-eye view of the gorge and surrounding rainforest.

Seconds later, after a gentle nudge or word of encouragement by a crewmember, they plunge 111 metres towards the raging river. Luckily, they are attached to the bridge by a bungee cord, strapped to their ankles! Other thrill seekers take up the offer to go even higher, while on microlight or helicopter tours over the falls. Every passenger on board our truck signed up for at least one activity, including the chance to go white-water rafting on the Zambezi.

After we'd set up our tents in a wooded campsite, Jeff led us on an evening walk into town for dinner at a local restaurant. During the gentle stroll, we passed a grass verge, splattered with fresh dollops of elephant dung, and came across two warthogs crossing the road. It seemed like one of those images where mankind and wildlife exist in harmony, often portrayed on the front cover of ecotourism magazines.

Throughout the meal, the major topic of discussion was the upcoming rafting trip on the Zambezi. By nightfall we were still buzzing with excitement, as we headed back to the campsite, our torchlights probing the darkness for signs of elephant dung on the track ahead.

Our trip started the following morning, with a short drive across the border into Zambia to meet the rafting team. The safety briefing was a sobering experience, as we quickly came to realise that we were not about to enjoy an amusement park ride. This was the real deal, with up to 500 million litres of water plummeting over the mile-wide falls each minute.

We'd begin our rafting trip close to the base of the falls and would need to be fully prepared to get bruised, battered, and wet. Five teams were selected, each with a boat leader. Our raft had the only female pilot licensed to take tours on the Zambezi, a confident young woman called Claire, blessed with sun-kissed hair and a Californian smile.

Fran and I were crewing with three English men, called Terry, Jim and Michael, who were tackling Africa without using a travel company. They'd purchased a Land Rover on one side of the continent and were now in transit to the other. During a lull in the safety talk, I spoke with Terry, a fair-haired boilermaker from Birmingham. I was keen to learn more about their self-managed trip, but Terry had other things on his mind and pointed towards one of his friends. 'Please watch out for Jim, as it was his birthday yesterday. The big three-oh. He's got a mighty hangover.'

Jim sat in the corner swigging a can of Coke, eyes glazed, oblivious to the safety talk. Before we dispersed, Claire called us together. While we sat close by, she quietly explained that the Zambezi is classified by the British Canoe Union as grade five. This ranking is given to rivers that are extremely difficult to kayak or raft, with long and violent rapids, steep gradients, big drops and pressure areas.

While she spoke, I glanced over at Jim. His eyes were closed, and he was rubbing his temples. She then pointed to a group of black men sitting at the back of the room, in quiet discussion together. 'Guys, take a look at those kayakers. They live and breathe the Zambezi and are some of the best in the world at what they do. Make sure you give them a wave as one of them may well save your life today.'

We glanced over and a few nodded back. They looked toned, relaxed and physically conditioned to daily life on the turbulent river. After our talk, we helped pack up the trailers with kayaks, inflatables, helmets, safety jackets and paddles, then headed to the river in convoy.

We soon entered a tropical paradise, filled with a myriad of plants, all a different shade of green. The air felt damp and cool, courtesy of the spray from the nearby falls. The wide leaves of nearby plants glistened in the early light as we unpacked the equipment next to a muddy trail that led through the jungle, towards the gorge.

I was handed a paddle, a helmet and the end of an eight-man inflatable, and told not to fall over. The weight of the raft helped to pull us down the steep slope, through the forest and into the canyon. Without warning or a cry for help, Jim dropped his section of the raft and dived into the forest. Despite the roar of millions of litres of water cascading over the lip of the falls, I could clearly hear the guttural sound of Jim, heaving his guts up.

David Livingstone is credited as being the first European to view the falls, while exploring parts of the Zambezi in 1855. Even in his wildest dreams, he surely couldn't have imagined that many years later, travellers from across the world would raft down the rapids on organised excursions. Upon sighting the falls, he wrote the following in his diary:

"No one can imagine the beauty of the view from anything witnessed in England. It had never been seen before by European eyes; but scenes so lovely must have been gazed upon by angels in their flight."

Although we were only a few hundred metres downriver of the falls, I didn't have the time to fully appreciate the awe-inspiring view. The first groups launched in quick succession without a hitch, prompting Claire to call us into action by rechecking our lifejackets. Such is the ferocity of the water that a loose jacket can easily be ripped off. If sucked under without a jacket, you are in deep trouble. Despite the dangers, tragic accidents involving rafters are rare, mainly due to the high safety standards of those that operate on the river.

The Zambezi, however, is a wild and unforgiving body of water. Flash flooding, unseasonal rains and unseen boulders lurking below the waterline can become major hazards. Capsized rafters have been sucked under the water and trapped between submerged rocks. Others have had close encounters with the crocodiles that inhabit calmer sections of the river. Then there is the washing machine effect, where those that have fallen overboard get caught in the turbulent water and continually spun around, hoping to be spat out before they run out of air!

With these thoughts in mind, I carefully listened to Claire's instructions as she moved us around the craft to balance the load. Two of the English lads were positioned in the front for maximum paddle power. One of these was Jim, and although he had broad shoulders and toned muscles, he didn't seem to be fully committed to the cause.

Our first mission was to break out of a small but lively eddy, which continually nudged us towards the shoreline. Despite our spirited efforts, we faltered on each occasion. As the raft bobbed sedately next to the bank, Claire stood up at the back, shouting to be heard over the noise of the thundering falls. 'Guys, what are you doing? This is utter crap! If you can't get out of this inlet, what will you be like on the river? You get one more go and if we don't break free, I'm calling it a day. I'm not risking my life for you bunch of wasters.'

She was right to be angry, as we were a pitiful, uncoordinated bunch. The three English lads were the key to our success, but Jim's pale features had gone unnoticed by Claire. He leant overboard to dunk his face in the water and emerged, dripping wet. He then let out a hearty war cry as we paddled hard to burst free of the inlet. Suddenly we were in unfamiliar terrain, with feisty waves pounding nearby rocks as we settled in our positions and searched the choppy water for signs of the first rapid.

We'd only been on the move for a few seconds, so I was surprised to hear Claire call out, 'Man overboard,' so quickly. I was even more surprised to turn around and see that Fran was missing from her spot. After a frantic search, I spotted her bright helmet in the water. She was heading towards distant boulders and Claire was bellowing out commands to steer us in the right direction. 'Right side–paddle hard,' she roared. 'Okay, now all of you go, go, go!'

Fran bobbed in and out of view, pushed involuntarily towards the first rapid, but Claire had read the current. She whipped in quickly to pluck her from the water, then turned sharply to avoid nearby rocks. The raft headed away from danger, permitting Claire to let out a whooping cry as she gave Fran a high five. As Fran scrambled back to her position in the raft, I made eye contact and got a shivery grin in return.

Despite our initial fears, the first two rapids were fun romps as the raft navigated the dips and swells. This all changed on rapid number three. By comparison, this was a monster, biting hard and fast as we struggled to find traction in the roar and turbulence. A freak surge tugged at my oar, spinning it full circle into the side of Terry's helmet. A split second later, our raft was forced vertical by a hidden boulder. Some of us tried hanging on, but the raft stalled in mid-air and began to twist. Apart from Claire, every other rafter was hurled into the angry slab of white-water.

At the mercy of the powerful force, we were temporarily sucked under, battered by rocks, and spat out at intervals. My paddle had vanished, but I knew it was essential to face the way I was heading. I leaned back and kept my legs high, to push off from the rocks as the pull of the water forced me through the canyon.

A kayaker raced into view, urging me to hug his bow with both arms and legs as we hurtled towards the imminent challenge of rapid number four, known as Morning Glory. He was now fully focused on hammering through the next rapid, and all I could do was hang on tight and enjoy the ride. The nose of the kayak ploughed deep into the water and for a fleeting moment I was completely submerged. Luckily, the bow was forced upwards by its buoyancy, which gave me valuable time to take a breath of air. The noise was deafening and there was little I could do except cling to the sides, as feisty waves slammed into me from every angle.

My arms and legs refused to surrender as this man, who I had never spoken to, steered me past thundering chasms, gaping holes and rounded boulders, towards the comparative safety of a rock pool. As I let go of the kayak, he smiled brightly and said, 'Well done, man. You were cool.'

I tried to talk, but the words were lost in a fit of coughs. Instead, I waved as he called out, 'Hey man, I've gotta go. Stay here for Claire.'

Without another word, he set off downriver, carving his paddle through the choppy waters with professional ease. Claire appeared from upstream, riding solo on the raft, and we waited in the safety of the pool while our crewmembers floated into view. Fran's smile told me all was well, but as Jim was pulled onto the raft, Claire heard his mild ramblings. He was moved to the rear, his place taken over by Michael.

Before we ventured to the next rapid, Claire gave us a pep talk. It started calmly enough, with words of encouragement about our progress so far. She pointed to a few of us and gave advice on how to improve our technique. Then the tone of her voice changed as her eyes narrowed. 'Listen up everyone. This is important. So far, we've been in a kindergarten. The next rapid is grade five. It's the real deal and is called Stairway to Heaven. It bites and if you get bitten, you may get hurt. It has killed and will kill again.'

Once again, the departing words of my mother-in-law came to mind: "*Don't do anything silly and please look after Fran.*"

Fran was by my side, grinning mischievously. In contrast, my stomach was in knots as Claire called out once more. 'Listen carefully. If you fall in, you might get sucked under–maybe for ten seconds. Believe me, it will seem far longer! Check your lifejackets are tight. Extra tight! If they come off, you may be sucked under for good.'

There was a clatter of noise as each passenger double checked their own lifejacket and then did the same for their partner. Once complete, all eyes were on Claire as she gave the next instructions. 'When we enter the rapid, you'll see a mass of foaming water protecting a wide slab of rock. We don't want to be pulled towards there. If we do, we flip. If we flip, you may get sucked under and trapped underneath. Kiss your ass goodbye if that happens, as it's near impossible to escape. When I give the call, paddle like there is no tomorrow. Paddle like your very life depends on it. Paddle like the devil is on your shoulder. Does anyone here not understand the importance of the next few minutes of our lives?'

She was met by silence and nodding heads. 'Good, then let's go. And remember–have fun and don't muck this up.'

Claire positioned the boat in the middle of the river and stood tall at the back, to pick out the best spot for the approach. While calling for us to keep paddling, she steered us into a gulley of fast water that propelled us forward at increasing speed. Suddenly, we could hear the train coming and there was no escape! Within seconds, the raft was sucked into a powerful channel and spat into the air as we dropped towards an untamed belly of glistening boulders and angry whirlpools.

We pitched awkwardly upon landing, but stayed afloat as each of us furiously paddled. The main boulder loomed closer as we hurtled towards the gaping hole at its base, but Claire pitched hard on the rudder at the last second. She timed our move to perfection, sweeping us away from the roaring pit of white froth and out of danger.

Wild screams erupted from the crewmembers as we yelled and punched the air in a mixture of excitement and relief. Claire took the initiative and dived straight into the next set of rapids. The boat flipped instantly at rapid eight. Hidden rocks forced the raft vertical, and every passenger was spun into the air. Claire had just passed a five-metre whirlpool called Star Trek and we were spat out of its wake.

The upturned craft hammered along the surface, with Claire clinging to the top and all others scattered throughout the river. I surfaced underneath the raft and scrambled for a hold in the darkness. While in the air pocket, a voice called out alongside me, but I had no idea who it was. Initially, the words were drowned out by the surge of water, but during a quieter stretch I recognised the voice. It was Jim, screaming for help. 'I'm here. I'm under the boat. Claire, get me out. I can't breathe.'

There was little I could do to help. I clung to a handhold and yelled at Jim to do the same, but he never replied. Claire's voice broke through the thunderous roar, urging him to stay calm. He went quiet and together we hurtled blindly past unseen boulders. During the commotion, my thoughts turned to Fran, hoping she was safe. I had no control and waited until the rapid spat us out.

Claire flipped the boat at the next rock pool and one by one our crew floated downriver to join us. I spotted Fran, still smiling as she clambered onto nearby rocks to take a breath. Jim was seated nearby, surrounded by his two friends. He was clearly suffering, but our location was remote and outside help was difficult to come by. Claire passed him a bottle of water and watched as he took tentative sips. As soon as he'd found his voice and managed a smile, she pulled him up and patted his back. 'Hey buddy, the hardest part is over. Well done.'

Rapid nine, named Commercial Suicide, is rated grade six and we left it well alone. While taking a wide berth, each of us helped carry the raft and equipment past the deafening roar of turbulent water. Above the noise, Claire pointed out the best line of attack for the snarling white jaws. She also mentioned that only the best kayakers in the world take on the epic challenge, with no guarantee of success.

By now, the sun was dropping, which signalled the end of our trip on the river. During the last few rapids of the day, Michael and Terry rode upfront, arms held high in anticipation of each surge. Jim tentatively paddled alongside Claire, and Fran continued grinning until we pulled over to the riverbank.

Two hours later we were back at the headquarters for the rafting company, feasting on spicy chilli. I hunted down my rescuer, who shrugged off any accolades but accepted the well-earned beers. We stayed longer than planned, sucked into the euphoria, toasting our guides and reliving the spills. By nightfall, Jim's colour had returned to his freckled cheeks, as he stood alongside a makeshift bar with Terry, Michael and Claire, each with a drink in hand and a story to tell.

I'd miss the English lads. They were good fun and reminded me of the friends I'd left behind in England. As we sped along the dark highway towards the border with Zimbabwe, I tried to work out where some of them would be at this time. But my thoughts were cloudy, and I couldn't find the mental strength to work out the time difference between Zambia and England. The Zambezi had left me battered and bruised. After too many celebratory beers, all I craved now, was sleep.

Fran woke me the following morning with the promise of a cooked breakfast of eggs and bacon. I stirred to life and tried opening my eyes. Overnight, one of them had swelled and my head throbbed with the pain. To complicate matters, I was also shivering and could hardly find the strength to climb out of the sleeping bag. I shrugged off any talk about doctors and rolled over, eager to sleep. The fever lasted for a day and night, leaving me weak and tender as I emerged from the tent in search of breakfast. I finally got the chance to enjoy eggs and bacon, followed by a walk into the nearby forest.

The winding trail led us towards the top of the falls, with numerous places to stop and admire the continual surge of water pouring over the wide escarpment into the deep gorge. Through a gap in the trees, we spotted Devil's Pool, a natural infinity pool with a difference. It is located so close to the edge of the waterfall, that it's possible to bathe in the pool and look down at the slab of angry water, 108 metres below.

There were several holidaymakers in the pool, who'd swam across from a nearby island with guides. All that stopped them from tumbling over the sheer side, towards a probable death, was a narrow lip of rock. We watched as they posed for photos at the top of the falls, chaperoned by their guides, who stood nearby, one step from the perilous edge.

It wasn't just the deafening roar of water, the fearless holidaymakers and brave guides that captured our attention, but the abundance of trees, birds and insects. It felt as though we were in the Garden of Eden. I wanted to stay for longer, but our time was nearly up, with an early morning departure planned for the following day. With this thought in mind, we headed into town for provisions.

By late afternoon, after a successful shopping spree, we were seated in an internet café, reading an unwanted email that threatened to put a dent in our plans. After our trip across southern Africa, we planned to move to Australia. We'd already lodged an application and had signed up the services of a migration consultant to manage the entire process. Although his fees were high, we decided it would be worth the expense, considering we'd be out of the country on a worldwide trip. We'd met him before our trip to Africa began, in a cramped office in London.

During the meeting, we'd explained that Fran had previously worked in Romania for two years, as a volunteer with an orphanage. He'd dismissed this information because the skilled visa application was in my name. As far as he was concerned, Fran's time in Romania was irrelevant and he shrugged away the offer to take copies of her paperwork. As we were paying a premium for his expertise, we'd assumed he was right and forgot all about the matter.

Now it seemed the Australian Government was more interested than our migration agent, concerning Fran's time in Romania. They wanted a police clearance from the Romanian authorities to prove she was not wanted for any criminal activities. Until then, our visa process was stalled. All paperwork regarding her time in Romania was rolling around in a container ship, somewhere between England and Australia.

We could either wait to get our hands on the paperwork and then sort out the problem via phone calls to Romania. From experience, Fran knew this would be near impossible. The agent also sensed this. His email gave a recommendation, for Fran to travel to Romania to speed up the process, as we only had so much time before our application expired.

It was evident that our agent had made a mistake, and I was keen to let him know. With no public phones, we convinced a local bungee jump operator to loan us his landline and got through to London on the first attempt. I recognised his voice at once, despite the crackle in the line. 'Hello, how may I help?'

'My name is Alistair and I'm calling—'

'Oh, I'm so glad you called, Alistair, as I've been trying to get hold of you. Don't you answer your phone or read emails?'

'Of course, but if you remember, I'm travelling through Africa with my wife before moving to Australia.'

'It's your wife that is the problem, it seems.'

'Yes, I've read the email and I'm a bit confused. When you checked over our application forms, you strongly insisted that her paperwork wasn't necessary.'

There was a moment of silence, followed by a cough. 'We have to deal with the facts as they are now, Alistair, not cling to the past.'

'Well, here's a fact for you. According to your email, my wife needs to fly to Romania during a European winter, rather than to Sydney with me to enjoy an Australian summer.'

'That's correct, Alistair. Unless you try to sort it out when your documents arrive by ship. Without a police clearance, your visa application is now on hold.'

I tightened my grip on the phone and asked, 'Can you please confirm who will pay for this oversight?'

As the line went silent, I thought he'd offer something to help me out. I wasn't after much. An apology would have been enough. When he next spoke, the manner and tone of his words were brisk and businesslike. 'I suggest you get off the phone and search for a cheap flight to Romania, rather than arguing with me.'

I could feel the heat in my cheeks, but tried to remain calm. 'Why didn't you tell us before we left for Africa? What exactly did you do to earn our fee? Can you at least admit you made a mistake?'

My questions were met with silence, so I spoke again. 'Hello, is anyone there?'

His smooth voice was soft and clear. 'Please let me know when she has the police clearance. If there is nothing else, I have to go.'

'Actually, there is something else.' I let loose with a burst of obscenities and hung up. The bungee operator took the phone from my shaking hand and pocketed the dollars I left on the counter.

Changes

"Wilderness without wildlife is just scenery."
Lois Crisler

By the time we returned to camp a handful of passengers were packing to leave. Chris was one of them, which saddened me a little, as I'd gotten used to our daily chats on the truck as we wound our way south. He was returning to London, with the chance of a promotion on the cards. There were three others leaving, all good friends, who'd proved inseparable throughout the trip. Despite various efforts by most other passengers, they'd rarely joined in with the festivities or banter.

I watched as they walked past, laden down with heavy rucksacks, their minds on the next destination instead of a farewell gesture. I met Chris at the camp reception, waiting for a shuttle bus, surrounded by his luggage and mementos. He held a large wooden carving of a giraffe in one hand, and with the other, reached out to shake my hand. 'This time next week, the giraffe will be pride of place by my lounge window and I'll wonder if this trip was all a dream.'

I wished him good luck and set off to find Fran, but after a few steps he called me back. 'You know, Alistair, I've often thought about the altercation you had with Troy when you first came on board. Until then, none of us had changed seats since leaving Nairobi. I noticed how you and Fran moved around from time to time, getting to know us all, including Troy.'

Then he smiled and said, 'If I did it all again, I think I'd also move seats occasionally. I guess the seat with the buzzer is free, if you still want it!'

After another handshake, I left him with his giraffe and headed towards the tents, my thoughts on Troy. His childish outbursts had reduced over the weeks, maybe because he no longer shocked anyone. I'd tried chatting with him during some evenings over a beer, but rarely managed to raise a smile. Overland trips test us all, I suppose. Lots of characters, opinions and egos thrown together, for weeks on end, far away from home while living side by side. Add romance to the mix, along with religion, personal interests, politics, upbringing and nationality, and you create an interesting smorgasbord.

The only recent additions to the passenger list were a couple from Australia. The guy came over and we shook hands. He was tall, with trimmed hair and a friendly handshake. 'G'day, mate, Wayne's the name. This is my girlfriend, Naomi.'

Naomi was petite, with curly brown hair and an infectious smile. She softly shook hands and within seconds started chatting with Fran. They'd been in the UK for a few years on working visas and had met whilst in London. Wayne was from Queensland and Naomi from Western Australia. Although they were both from the same country, the distance between their home states is similar to the gap between London and Moscow!

They were on their way to Perth, Western Australia, and had decided on an overland adventure across southern Africa to break up the journey. After the introductions, Wayne called me to one side. 'What's the deal with the Aussies that are leaving the tour? None of them are smiling. Don't worry, mate, we're not all miserable bastards, you know.'

Our final evening in Zimbabwe started with sundowners by the pool. Wayne and Naomi reinstated Australians' reputations as beer-swilling, fun-loving, party animals. I was really beginning to enjoy life as an overlander!

Low clouds greeted us the next morning as we quietly packed our damp tents into the truck. Breakfast was a rushed affair, with all thoughts on the gathering clouds, rather than the sizzling bacon and fried eggs on offer. Throughout the morning, we sped through several showers and the occasional squall. Towns and villages came and went, but very few passengers gazed outside to study them.

By midday, the sides of the truck were rolled down to shield us from the wind and rain. Music was cranked high and beers flowed as we drove along the main road, to cross the border into an unseasonably boggy Botswana. Our destination was Chobe National Park, renowned for its impressive elephant population, estimated at 100,000. Over dinner, we met with one of the camp rangers. He was neatly dressed in khaki shorts, a matching top, and stout walking boots. After apologising about the weather, he then gave a detailed rundown of the following day's plan. It would be a pre-dawn start, as rain was expected later in the day.

As promised, we set off just before the sun made its appearance, each of us rugged up to fend off a chill wind that promised rain. The clouds played cat and mouse all morning, as we wound our way along well-worn bush tracks, in search of wildlife. We were on board an open-topped Land Rover, which offered far-reaching views of the open grassland. Vibrant bee-eaters darted in the cool breeze as we headed towards a vast floodplain, inhabited by a herd of antelope.

A crack of timber broke the spell and all heads turned as one, to admire the two elephants that had come into view from an area of scrubland. The calf kept close to mum, who seemed unperturbed by our presence, as she continued her line of travel towards the vehicle. She stopped and raised her mottled trunk to explore our scent. The inquisitive calf was gently pushed under her belly where it obediently stayed, wrapping its narrow trunk around mum's leg. The mother reached out with her trunk, gently caressing the driver's door as we watched in silence. From the back seat, Fran whispered, 'Can we please go now?'

The elephant's ears flapped and she slowly backed off, guiding her calf towards a line of trees. Within minutes, they'd vanished from sight. With so many elephants in Chobe, it wasn't hard to spot many more, including a herd of cape buffalo, which we sighted alongside a shallow waterhole.

We watched for a while as they stood hoof-deep in the mud, drinking at intervals before lifting their heavy heads to study the terrain. One looked to be jittery, shaking its head from side to side, before taking a few steps towards us. We were still relatively far away, but the movement triggered a reaction from our driver, who eased the Land Rover away from the waterhole.

A few minutes later, while on the search for more animals, the driver called out, 'We weren't in danger, but they can be unpredictable. They are majestic beasts for sure, but those *dagga boys* will gorge a hole in you if ever they feel threatened.'

Initially, I thought the word dagga referred to the wide horns of the buffalo, but the driver explained it was a Zulu term for mud. Evidently, buffalos enjoy nothing better than a muddy pool of water to wallow in, and with heavy rains forecast overnight, there would soon be plenty of puddles to choose from.

Overland trucks don't sit still for long and the following morning we left behind the grey skies, crossed into Namibia and headed along the Caprivi Strip, a narrow stretch of land that extends along its north-eastern border. Its proximity to Angola makes some travel companies cautious, even though the civil war is now history. This vast area once suffered from extensive poaching, partly due to the hostilities and lack of governance. Nowadays, it is hoped that the remote environment and political stability can aid its recovery into the natural oasis it once was. Regardless of the wild and isolated land on either side of the long straight road, Tony drove non-stop, as he was keen to reach our campsite before sunset.

Once again, I sat beside him on the journey and as the miles tumbled, he shared his reasons for escaping the rat race. After years of frustration while driving lorries between Britain and mainland Europe, he'd traded a stressful and repetitive existence for an adventurous life. Instead of worrying about traffic jams, ferry queues, industrial action, winter storms and French blockades (at least once per year, he informed me with a smile), his life was now so much simpler. From what I could see, it was also far more exciting.

I'd studied him during the past few weeks and could see that he was proud of the way he meticulously maintained the truck. While tents were being unpacked, he'd complete a daily ritual of checking tyres, oil, brakes and other essential components. Once finished, he could often be found in the corner of the bar, enjoying a cold beer with his wife. Occasionally, he'd get called over to join a raucous group with their drinking games, but being older than most, you somehow knew that he'd seen and done it all before. Most times he'd politely smile and decline their offer, but occasionally he'd join in for a while, before stealing away.

I didn't know it at the time, but this was to be one of my last trips in the front cab with Tony. Other passengers were vying for a chance to enjoy the bird's-eye view and friendly chats. As our next camp approached, I asked the inevitable question. 'So Tony, with all that you've seen and experienced, where's your favourite place in Africa?'

He took a while to reply, his south London accent somehow out of place as we passed a warning sign for hippos. 'There are still many places for me to explore in Africa. I enjoy every trip, as each is different in some way. You sometimes meet a group of passengers that make the trip a memorable one and at other times it's a wildlife experience that takes your breath away. I love the remoteness of Malawi and the wilds of Tanzania. As for my favourite camping spot, it could well be Ngepi, which is where we'll be very soon!'

He reached towards the sun visor, pulled out an assortment of leaflets and asked me to find the one on Ngepi. I flicked through the material, suddenly aware of all the other locations and attractions that could be visited during a tour of Africa. I found the one on Ngepi and read the first lines: *Ngepi camp is situated in the unspoiled upper reaches of the Okavango Delta panhandle, in the western Caprivi strip, Kavango Region, Namibia.*

While I studied the leaflet, Tony informed me about the prolific wildlife that could be found in the area, including elephant, buffalo and leopard. The remaining words on the flyer completed the picture:

With clean Kalahari Desert air, the camp is set on an island under amazing trees, with permanent river frontage and surrounded by seasonally flooded swamps. It is a paradise of flooded plains and secret swampy backwaters, teeming with wildlife. We are nestled between Mahango National Park a few kms to the south and Bwabwata National Park, directly opposite across the river.

As I handed back the leaflet, the welcome sign for Ngepi came into view, prompting Tony to drop through the gears, before taking a dirt track that led towards the entrance. Up ahead, a parked truck signalled that we would not be alone. Located nearby, under the shade of a tree, were two Land Rovers, their wheels and paintwork lightly coated in red dirt.

With just a few hours until sunset, all passengers were eager to stretch their legs and explore the grounds. We soon discovered a wide strip of grass, which led towards the water's edge. It was dotted with tents and some campers had strung makeshift washing lines between the trees. Their dried clothes hung lifeless in the warm air as we dropped our packs on vacant spaces, to claim a resting place for the night.

Nearby, we spotted a series of wooden huts, positioned snugly in the branches of tall trees. Each treehouse offered far-reaching views towards the river. For those without a tent or a head for heights, there was also the option to stay in a selection of wooden cabins, each with a private garden and open-air bathroom.

Instead of such luxuries we had our dome tents, which we pitched close to the shade of jackalberry trees; each one laden with ripening fruit. Birds and insects ruled the skies, forever darting in and out of view, each a different shape, colour and sound to the last. One passenger sat cross-legged on the grass, binoculars held to his eyes, and wildlife guidebook close by.

After we'd set up our tents, Jeff called a meeting. We met inside the camp restaurant, a large A-framed wooden structure, protected by a straw-lined roof. Pride of place belonged to a polished slab of hardwood, positioned close to the far wall and used as the bar. The skull of an antelope adorned one wall and to complete the theme, the reed-lined walls were adorned with a flag of Namibia and an adult sized map of Africa.

A few guests from another overland truck were sitting around a nearby table, playing cards. Most looked to be in their late twenties and all had tanned faces. One man raised his beer glass, before calling out a greeting. They had the relaxed look of those that had lazed away the day in hammocks, rather than the back of an overland truck on a bumpy road. A few days earlier they'd probably have rolled into camp and sat through a similar speech to the one that Jeff was about to deliver to us.

He was seated at the bar and called out for silence. 'Hi guys, listen up for a few minutes as I have a few things to discuss.'

As the room fell silent, I turned to Wayne and lowered my voice. 'Can you remember how many nights we're here for? I hope it's longer than I think it is.'

'Ali, I'm not sure, but I reckon we're about to find out. I heard earlier that we're going to be offered the chance to head into the Okavango Delta, for a night or two.'

As Wayne signalled to the barman for two beers, I returned my attention to Jeff's presentation. Although we'd only just arrived, I sensed we'd found somewhere special to stay and the thought of breaking camp so soon, seemed ludicrous.

As a few last-minute stragglers entered the back of the room, Jeff raised his voice to be heard. 'So, as you can see, this place is pretty special. The staff are passionate about the environment and they expect you to respect the rules. There aren't many, but the ones they have are there for a reason. Although you'll have access to fresh water, limited solar power and plenty of cold drinks, don't forget that you are smack in the middle of the African wilderness. Please don't get complacent, just because it has a great-looking bar, toilets with a view, funky showers and a riverside setting for the tents.'

He then pointed outside, towards the wide river. 'Just to be clear of the dangers, a local woman was recently mauled by a crocodile while washing her clothes by the riverbank. She's going to be okay, but last week the camp owner's dog was not so lucky. The golden rule is to have fun, remain vigilant and go easy on the drinks.'

All eyes turned towards Horse, as Jeff smiled at him and said, 'That means you, too!'

Horse raised a beer into the air and smiled, while Jeff continued. 'Watch out for hippos and make sure you don't get caught between them and the water. They'll feel threatened, you might get chomped and my insurance premium will go up!'

To a chorus of laughter, he then said, 'That's the end of the serious stuff. Let me know who wants to take an excursion into the Okavango Delta. It's the trip of a lifetime, so I suggest you think seriously about it, even though Ngepi is too good a place to leave. I'll chat with you all later, to confirm the numbers.'

After the talk, I set off with Fran, to explore the camp and get our bearings. We discovered open air toilets with western style seats, offering views fit for a king. The thrones were screened by reeds and reached by a series of wooden steps. Those doing their business did so with a panoramic outlook over the trees and river. It was clear that the owners had a sense of humour, with a scattering of unusual signs located across the camp. One in the bar was inscribed with the words: *Our staff are friendly but the hippos are not!*

By the time we reached the river, the setting sun had worked its magic on the wide-open sky, adding a touch of colour to each passing cloud. While photographers searched for the perfect angle, I spotted dark shapes in the river. I could see the heads of each hippo and counted ten of them together, before a high-pitched scream grabbed my attention.

One guest was in mid-air, wearing bright trunks and a wide smile. A second later, he splashed into the river and was soon joined by his friends. There was no need to panic, as they'd leapt from a wooden platform, housed inside a purpose-built pontoon, known as the *croc cage*. Tethered to the bank and protected on all sides (including the bottom), the square shaped float proved to be a popular haunt for those wishing to cool off in relative safety. Close by, I found another sign. *Please don't pee in the water as you'll be drinking it later in your coffee.*

Sometime later, hunger tempted most of us away from the riverbank, towards the restaurant. Music spilled into the warm night air as travellers from across the world shared stories. The smell of grilled meat wafted through the open-air bar, where I sat with Fran, alongside a middle-aged couple that had arrived a few days earlier by Land Rover. After many weeks away from their home in Cape Town, this was to be the furthest point of their journey. By morning, they'd be heading towards the coast before making their way south.

As the evening wore on, apart from one male guest deciding to undertake an impromptu streak across the floor, most were happy enough to dance the night away fully clothed! Sometime later, we ventured outside and carried on dancing under the stars, until at last, time was called.

During our walk towards the scattering of tents, we heard frantic voices calling for help. We soon discovered that Horse had gone missing and grabbed some torches to join the search party. We found him by the riverbank, snoring softly, while lying flat on his back in the long grass. By the time he was tucked up safely, the camp had fallen silent.

Back in our tent we settled down for the night, lying in the pitch black, wrapped inside our sleeping bags. Somewhere in the distance, an owl hooted, and crickets chirped softly in the still air. We chatted quietly about the fun night, our words slurred, and gradually all conversation ceased. I woke sometime later, my thoughts too groggy to understand the source of the loud grunts coming from far away. I lay for a while, still sleepy, and began to drop off again, just as the noises returned. This time, the grunts were closer and far louder.

My senses sharpened, and I quietly groped in the dark for a torch. Fran stirred, but I left the torch off and listened again. The crickets had gone silent. I sat upright to concentrate fully and heard the faint sound of grass being ripped from the earth. Fran woke with a jolt, but before she had the chance to speak, I whispered in her ear. 'Shh, there are hippos outside.'

One was getting nearer, its grunts now very close, and we sat rigid as it passed the doorway and scraped its body along the side of our tent. A foot caught on a rope, pulling it from the earth, and one side of the canvas sagged. By the doorway, another hippo belched loudly and munched the sweet grass. I then heard Fran's hushed voice, as she reached out for my hand. 'What do we do?'

My reply was just as quiet. 'Do you remember what Jeff said? The best thing to do right now is absolutely nothing. Inside the tent we're safe.'

We settled back into our sleeping bags and listened to the hippos as they trampled through the campsite. Eventually, the belches and grunts blended in with the sound of the returning crickets, and we fell into a deep sleep.

Ghost Town

"A diamond is forever."
Mary Frances Gerety

By late morning we were travelling by speedboat to the edge of the Okavango Delta. Local guides were waiting to transport us along the crystal-clear channels on traditional canoes, known as *mokoros*. The speedboat could not outrun a churning mass of black clouds, which hit us mid-way through an open lagoon. Lightning crashed into the forest, followed by trumpets of thunder and thick drops of rain that lashed against our small craft. The storm receded as we reached our destination, a small brick building, hidden behind reeds.

Positioned neatly on the embankment sat a row of wooden mokoros. Our guide advised us that silence and a keen eye were the key to appreciating the experience. With this valuable strategy, he pushed off from the banks with a long wooden pole and transported us to paradise! Papyrus reeds towered over us as we glided through the clear waters. At each turn, we discovered small lagoons, adorned with speckled-green lily pads. A dragonfly darted across the millpond, hovering close to us for valuable seconds. In the blink of an eye, it sped away, replaced by another.

The waterway narrowed in places, causing us to duck as we brushed past giant leaves before arriving at the next lagoon. We had no clue to what lay ahead and stayed silent, hoping we might encounter large animals. Elephants had been spotted the previous day and all eyes were peeled. A while later, we lay back in the narrow boats, watching birds in flight, while the guides punted us through the shallow channels.

The afternoon was spent in a sensual daze, with meandering treks across low-lying islands. No one spotted elephants, but few seemed bothered. We were just happy to walk quietly alongside our guides, who continually watched the way ahead. At times, I sensed they were wary that we'd stumble upon hippos. We got up close to open-billed storks and watched as they waded through the shallows in search of fresh-water mussels, ignoring the chatter from white-faced ducks that nested nearby.

Before dusk we made camp on an elevated parcel of land, by draping tarpaulins over branches to form a rooftop. We then lay our sleeping bags alongside each other and gathered wood for a fire. While enjoying homemade stew, the sun dipped below the horizon, coating the lingering clouds in a velvety sheen, and our world turned to darkness.

We lay flat on our backs, gazing into space. In the silence that followed, my eyes were drawn to the myriad of stars, calling for our attention. With no light pollution, we were spoiled for choice on where to look. Some passengers pointed out constellations, while others asked for silence as they searched for shooting stars. One stargazer spotted a satellite in orbit, the tiny white speck inching its way across the darkness. I realised then, as I stared deep into space, that it was proving harder each day to escape from the modern world. As I lay next to Fran, a song came to mind, written by the English musician, Billy Bragg. I started to quietly sing the words, as I probed the darkness for one more sighting of a meteor.

'I saw two shooting stars last night
I wished on them but they were only satellites
Is it wrong to wish on space hardware?
I wish, I wish you'd care.'

Fran overheard and came up with the idea of a fireside singalong. Her timing proved perfect as the mosquitoes were biting and we'd been called to the fire to enjoy hot tea. While sitting back from the flames, we formed groups according to nationality and picked traditional songs that reminded us of home. The Kiwis gave a passionate display of the 'Haka', followed by a belting rendition of 'Waltzing Matilda' by the Australians. The British contingent managed a half-hearted attempt at a children's nursery rhyme, called 'Old MacDonald'.

Our river guides disappeared into the bush to prepare, then slowly emerged to re-enact an ancient elephant hunt. One guide had tied a sprig of leaves around his head and crept behind the dwindling fire. His soft voice carried across the campsite as he mimicked a male elephant, searching for food. A hunter emerged from the darkness armed with a spear, his lean features contorted by the light of the flames. He crept towards the feasting elephant and stabbed at the shadows. The elephant collapsed, and the hunter danced in celebration, his arms thrust towards the stars. He then began chanting, so that the spirit of the noble beast would be released.

A dawn start was required to get back to Ngepi campsite. The rising sun carpeted the delta in a kaleidoscope of pink as we stood on the edge of the island. Our guides paddled into view, their dark silhouettes a contrast to the blaze of vibrant colour bursting across the waking horizon. No one wanted to leave, but we had to, and by noon we bade farewell to our guides. We all agreed that one night in the Okavango Delta was not enough.

Our last day at Ngepi was spent relaxing at camp. Some tried out the croc pool, others signed up for a river safari, and a few lounged in hammocks. During the afternoon, I went in search of Horse and found him in the camp bar. While ordering two beers, I heard excited voices and looked towards the entrance. A new group of arrivals had made it to Ngepi. Horse raised his glass and called out a greeting, just as their guide began his welcome speech.

We broke camp the following morning and headed west, towards Etosha National Park, 600 kilometres away. Covering over 20,000 square kilometres across an arid landscape, it could be wrongfully described as the world's largest sandpit. The benefit of lots of sand is that the wildlife is often drawn to the waterholes, unless of course it's the wet season. Although the wet season was officially over, we arrived during a late afternoon shower. The rain eased, but only to a drizzle, which put a damper on any thoughts of a campfire.

The ghostly figures of jackals could faintly be seen through the evening mist while we sat alongside the truck, enjoying a hastily cooked meal. If there was a camp bar, very few joined Horse in his quest to find it. Most were tucked up in their tents by nightfall and only a few of us heard the distant growls of prowling lions, before falling into a deep sleep.

The lethargy continued the following morning, even though we woke to clear skies. For three hours, we scouted regular waterholes and game tracks. We spotted herds of gazelle and zebra and stumbled across a pair of jackals lazing by a tree. Despite the occasional wildlife sighting, our enthusiasm eventually waned, due to hunger and thirst.

Wayne remained vigilant throughout and stirred us into action with the sighting of a male lion resting in the shade of an acacia tree. The lion stood and shook his mane, flicking red dirt into the air while stepping out of the shadows to investigate the murmurs coming from our truck. We instantly fell silent as his wild eyes calmly studied our animated faces. He was bigger than I first envisaged, with a muscular frame and long darkened tail. As we watched from up high, he moved slowly but purposely from left to right, leaving firm prints in the red earth. He then picked up speed and headed towards the nearest trees. Within seconds, apart from the indents in the sand, it was as though he'd never been there at all.

Back at camp, a watering hole attracted a steady supply of thirsty wildlife throughout the day. While appreciating the serenity of a protected lookout, I sat quietly alongside Fran to enjoy the comings and goings. The highlight was an unexpected event, caused by a brave jackal that continually tried to nudge a pair of rhinos away from a patch of shade.

After leaving the protected sanctuary of Etosha, the truck entered the stark reality of modern Namibia. Most land surrounding the national park seemed to be used for cattle farms, or private game reserves. We passed pockets of woodland and large tracts of savannah, but the land had been divided by barbed wire and sturdy fences. There didn't seem to be any natural corridors where migratory animals could move freely between the reserves.

As we travelled south, the land became drier, flatter and less populated, until we sighted a series of granite peaks, far in the distance. We were entering an area known as Spitzkoppe, where gravel plains give way to jagged hills. One of the most prominent peaks is 1,784 metres high and due to its steep sides and triangular shape, has attracted the nickname of the Matterhorn of Africa.

After we'd set up camp, three of the passengers marched across the desert floor towards the nearest peak. Wayne was one of them and as the sun dropped lower, I studied their progress through binoculars. Although hampered by a scattering of giant boulders surrounding the peak, they managed to navigate to the steep sides.

Some gained a foothold, but not for long. Without ropes and a guide, their quest for the summit fell short. They arrived back at sunset to a round of applause, and I handed Wayne a well-earned beer. The merriment continued, with a bottle of wine appearing on the scene, along with more beers.

During our evening meal, Fran suggested we escape from the party, to sleep under the stars. Earlier, we'd discovered a small hollow on top of a granite mound, 40 metres high. It looked like an ideal location for a night of solitude and after dinner we said goodnight to Wayne and Naomi, then clambered up the side. Our pack was filled with sleeping bags, blankets, water, torches and late-night snacks.

After checking the hollow for any nocturnal desert dwellers, we lay side by side, wrapped in a swathe of blankets. A cool breeze tugged at Fran's hair and helped to mask all sounds from the boisterous campsite, far below. Once again, we tracked satellites and counted meteors burning up across the night sky. There was no need for snacks, as we soon fell asleep to the sound of the wind, drifting across the desert. A gentle stroke of sunlight woke us, followed minutes later by a visit from Wayne. 'G'day, guys. It's time for breakfast and we're on the road in an hour.'

During our descent towards the campsite, Fran and Wayne discussed the notion of going on a morning run. After consulting with Tony and Jeff, they made plans to set off 30 minutes before the truck departed. As they prepared to leave, I raced ahead to get a photo of them in motion. While catching my breath, they arrived on the scene, the rising sun casting their long shadows across the gravel track. With each purposeful stride, they kicked up red dirt as they jogged past me with smiles and waves. Within minutes, the desert had swallowed them up.

I felt a pang of jealousy as I watched them go, but knew I wouldn't be able to keep up. Running was Fran's passion and Wayne seemed like a natural athlete. They'd been instructed to stay with each other and to keep on track, no matter what. There was little chance of encountering any other traffic, and there were no villages or settlements nearby.

While returning to the campsite, my mind wandered back to a moment long before, when I'd been in Tanzania with Owen. We'd also asked for permission to set off before the truck. Not to run, but to walk. We'd been in the countryside, close to farms and villages, but away from the game reserves. The road rarely stayed straight for long, as it weaved between small, rounded hills and passed alongside an expanse of trees. Just like Fran and Wayne, we made an early start and had been instructed to stay on the gravel track.

Along the way, we spotted wood smoke from distant settlements and sighted cattle grazing in faraway paddocks. During one long stretch, we passed close to a smallholding and heard a voice call out from the porch. 'Hello. Please come in for some tea!'

The voice sounded female, but we couldn't see anyone. We stopped by the road and peered towards the simple dwelling. A trail of smoke could just be seen, escaping from a narrow chimney, protruding through the tin roof of the cabin. There was a scattering of goats in an adjacent field and two children, standing in a dusty clearing, watching us with interest. One of them waved, just as we heard the female voice again. 'Please come in for tea.'

We were caught in a quandary. To be invited for early morning tea with strangers sounded exciting and a little daring. But to do so would mean leaving the road. The truck was due soon and would drive past without knowing we were at the settlement. Reluctantly, we decided to continue our journey. I called out, 'I'm sorry, but we have to go.'

That's when the lady appeared from her doorway and took a few steps towards us. She called out again, the same words, but louder. 'Please don't go. Come in for some tea.'

We waved goodbye, set off along the track, and waited for the truck to pick us up. It arrived a few minutes later, leaving a trail of dust in its wake.

I've often wondered what would have happened if we'd taken up the invitation for early morning tea. Moments like these, when on long journeys, often happen when least expected. Sometimes you can take them up and other times you have to let them go.

It was Tony that pulled me from the daydream, calling my name as I approached the truck. He asked if I wanted to sit up front, to help spot Fran and Wayne. I snapped up the offer, then went in search of leftovers as the passengers prepared to leave camp.

Our departure time took longer than planned and the sun was already biting by the time Tony started the engine and headed south. From up high, I could see the road as it split the desert in two. In places we passed a handful of hardy shrubs, peeking from the base of sun-baked rocks, but there were no trees or natural features to draw the eye.

It was Tony that spotted them first. From afar, they were just two blurred dots, lost in the haze. We caught up with them by a slight bend in the road. Both were red faced and glistening with sweat, but still going strong. Wayne with his long strides and Fran, ever competitive, by his side. Tony pulled over to the side of the road and they climbed on-board, to the sound of clapping. They both ignored the applause and asked instead, for water.

We then headed west, along a lonely road, surrounded by an expanse of sand and gravel. Hours later, we stepped off the truck and gazed at the cold, grey waters of the Atlantic Ocean. We were standing by the Skeleton Coast, which stretches for hundreds of kilometres towards the Angolan border and is littered with shipwrecks. Portuguese sailors began exploring the coastline of Africa during the 15th century and word soon spread about the unforgiving stretch of water that they termed, *The Gates of Hell.* If ever a ship became snarled on a coastal reef, the fate of the crew was all but sealed. Those that leapt into the cold water were at the mercy of rip currents, powerful waves, and razor-sharp rocks.

If any crewmembers made landfall, they were then faced with vast sand dunes, scorching daytime temperatures, and little chance of finding fresh water. To complete the picture, lions and hyenas often prowled the shoreline, in search of easy pickings.

Shipwrecks still occur, due to the strong cross currents, rocky reefs, and dense fog, which is known to appear without warning. The

San people, who once inhabited many parts of Namibia, referred to the coastline as, *The land that God made in anger*.

Tony handed me a pair of binoculars, pointed to the waves breaking close to shore, and asked me to search for shipwrecks. I found two in succession, one close to the beach and the other far off, broken into pieces and being pounded by the surf.

After stretching our legs, we boarded the truck and headed down the coast, towards Cape Cross, which is home to one of the largest colonies of cape fur seals in the world. There were thousands of them and most were huddled together on the rocks, between the water and the headland. During our walk towards the lookout point, we came across an elevated boardwalk, which gave us the chance to study the nearest seals from up high. They basked in the sunshine just below our feet, seemingly oblivious to the people walking past.

The water teemed with life, with seals continually heading in and out of the surf. Some passengers held their noses to ease the putrid smell of urine, faeces and rotting flesh. There was no way to avoid the noise. With males asserting their dominance and mothers calling for their young, the result was a constant din of chauvinistic grunts, competing with high-pitched yelps.

This was an untamed place. In such extreme conditions, the weak or young are easily trampled, and danger lurks in every direction. Great white sharks search beyond the reef for unwary seals, while hyenas scout the edge of the colony for those that stray too far. While heading back to the truck, I detoured towards the beach, but there was no sand to be found, only the rotted fragments of dead seals and fractured bones, bleached by the sun.

The only intrusion on nature was an abandoned brick building, advertised by a faded sign as a public convenience. The opportune sight of a toilet block triggered an unplanned call of nature. I ran through the open doorway, realising at once that the local shire had long since taken the building off their maintenance list.

The roof was all but gone, with no doors in any of the cubicles. Broken pipes revealed where a tap and basin had once been positioned, and out of the three cubicles, only one had a toilet. Surprisingly, it still had a seat, although this was cracked at the edges and ready to split in two. With hours until the next stop, I convinced myself that it would be worth dropping my pants, rather than being caught short while on the road.

Just before my bowels loosened, I heard a sound from the corridor. I called out, thinking it was a passenger from the truck, but there was no reply. The noise returned, this time closer. It sounded like something large and heavy, shuffling towards me across the sandy floor.

I stood quickly, pulling my pants up in one swift motion, just as the mystery guest arrived by the open doorway and let out a shrill bark. It was a juvenile seal, with a puppy face and snarling mouth, which revealed two rows of sharp teeth. It then shook its head from side to side and moved towards me into the narrow cubicle. In one swift movement, I ran towards the opening, sidestepping its snapping jaws, before racing into the corridor. The seal turned and gave chase, barking angrily as I raced outside, laughing at the folly and happy to have escaped.

It was time for some creature comforts, and with the coastal city of Swakopmund within reach, the timing was perfect. A sealed road led us through an undulating terrain, toasted by the sun and devoid of greenery. As Swakopmund drew closer, we no longer had the road to ourselves, with trucks, cars and motorbikes a common sight in both directions.

The city enjoys its status as the adventure capital of Namibia and is home to over 40,000 people. Sandwiched between the nutrient-rich waters of the Atlantic Ocean and the vast expanse of the Namib Desert, it's only natural that fishing and mining are two of the key industries that help support the local economy. It is also a premier tourist resort, renowned for its mild desert climate, seafood restaurants, expansive beaches and laid-back lifestyle.

After driving along a palm fringed highway, Tony was eventually forced to stop when faced with the first traffic lights we'd encountered since Bulawayo, in Zimbabwe, 1,800 kilometres away! While we waited at the red light, I leaned out of the truck to study the shopfronts. It didn't take long until I found one with a German name. Although the German army relinquished its control of Namibia in 1915, the city's colonial past is still evident, with a selection of ornate buildings, painted in bold colours, looking like they'd been transported from a Bavarian village.

Tony then drove us to an accommodation complex and within an hour, I was enjoying my first bath since leaving England! As Fran casually flicked through the TV channels, I soaked in the hottest water possible, trying hard not to feel guilty about taking a bath while in the Namib Desert. Over the next three days, we embraced the chance to sleep in a double bed, catch up on emails, and explore the town at a leisurely pace. Some passengers took long walks along the coastal footpath, returning hours later, flushed from the sun and exhilarated by the experience.

Fran and Naomi signed up to go tandem skydiving and after meeting their instructors were soon free-falling 12,000 feet above the desert. I teamed up with Wayne for a tamer excursion, to learn the basics of paragliding. After two swift lessons, we learnt how to launch solo from 100-metre dunes. Each flight lasted a few minutes, with panoramic views to the grey Atlantic and the vast dunes surrounding the city.

During the first evening, we raised steins filled with cloudy beer while working our way through a menu that included gastronomic delights such as bratwurst and pork schnitzel. Bloated by apple strudel, some passengers headed back to their apartments, while those with more stamina went in search of bright lights and loud music. On our second evening, Jeff announced it was his birthday and invited us all out for a meal. Even though most of us had signed up for an early morning sandboarding adventure, we danced into the early hours. Sometime after midnight, someone suggested a round of tequilas and by two in the morning, Fran was guiding me to our room.

I woke six hours later, groggy and confused. Fran was elbowing me in the ribs as there was someone knocking at the door. The guides had arrived to take us sandboarding, and with the sun growing stronger by the hour, time was of the essence. I could have said no and put the covers over my head. But Fran pushed me out of the bed, insisting I take photos, as she had a dental appointment and couldn't go.

No amount of caffeine could ease the pounding in my head, and the greasy egg burger that I scoffed down only added to the pains in my stomach. I took my second coffee into the quiet courtyard, contemplating an escape back to my room, but left the bid for freedom too late.

A hippy van containing a dazzling display of bleached hair, testosterone and tanned bodies tore into the car park, dragging with it an array of sandboards, crammed into a box trailer. Another minivan followed, driven by a red-eyed Nirvana fan, who clearly wanted Namibia to know he'd made it through another night. Once on board, I fled to the back seats and pulled my fleece tight around my eyes, ignoring the request for a high five from the guide.

It was Naomi who woke me on arrival and helped me off the minivan, which was now parked at the base of a dune. I'd forgotten my sunglasses and now paid the price, as blinding light reflected off the sand. As I shielded my eyes from the sun, our guide called us into a huddle to explain the technicalities of using snowboards on sand. During his speech, I had a flashback of downing tequilas with a group of German backpackers, the night before. My stomach retched, and I peeled away to scramble around in my daypack, for a water bottle that didn't exist.

My search was abandoned when Naomi called my name. We'd been assigned a task to carry some of the equipment to the top of the nearest hill, a 140-metre soft mound, known as Dune Seven. Large bottles of water were also required, and I stumbled over to grab one, before collecting snowboard boots and a board to haul up the waiting dune.

The group climbed onto the ridge, leaving me alone on the desert floor with one of the caskets. I drank greedily, savouring the sweet taste of Namibian spring water. I could have stayed longer, but partway through another gulp, Naomi appeared at the scene to escort me to the top. As we reached the pinnacle, I sat by the edge to catch my breath, enjoying each gulp of water while squinting into the sun. Our dune was one of thousands, each one carved from the winds. Some were taller, others were smaller, with no sign of greenery as far as the eye could see.

I spotted movement to my left, as our guide cruised by, carving through the searing sand while on a snowboard. He was calling out to the group to watch, so they could see how easy it was to do. As I struggled with my boots and board, the other day-trippers set off at intervals. Some made it look easy and managed to weave down the dune as though they were in the Alps on a winter's holiday. But the thrill was short-lived, with no ski lifts in sight. Instead, they had to trudge up the soft sand for their next attempt. Each one arrived at the top of the dune, red faced and gasping for water.

I'd been to the Alps many times before, to enjoy the snow. On each occasion I'd used skis, so for me this was a novel experience. What better place to learn snowboarding, then a 140-metre sand dune in Namibia, on a scorching day, while suffering from a hangover. After pushing off, I quickly gained speed, with no idea about how to stop. But I needn't have worried. As I tried to turn, the edge of the board dug into the soft sand, sending me cartwheeling down the slope. I landed head-first and open-mouthed into the warm, amber sands. Soon after, I limped from view, to recover in the shade of our minivan, while glugging from a discarded bottle of warm water.

After watching most of us fail, the guides collected narrow sheets of plywood from the trailer and explained they could be used like a sledge. Determined to glide down at least one dune unscathed I grabbed a piece of ply and climbed to the top for a second attempt.

Wayne and Naomi showed me the way, skimming down the steep slopes with ease while sitting on the plywood. I followed suit and managed my first smile of the morning as the wind whipped against my face. Using plywood needed little skill and delivered fast speed down the hard-packed ridges. Rising heat and a nagging thirst diminished the enthusiasm of the group and we headed back to town, with the sound of 'Smells Like Teen Spirit' pulsating from the minivan speakers.

After an early night, I woke refreshed, to take on the challenge of quad biking across the nearby dunes. Every other passenger signed up for the excursion and with a sense of anticipation we travelled to the edge of town to meet our tour guides. They were four local men in their 30s, who'd been quad biking for years and knew the terrain well. As they handed out helmets, gloves, and goggles, they asked if anyone had been quad biking before. As expected, they got a mixed response, from complete beginners to seasoned amateurs.

Their job was to ensure we all had the best time possible, with safety forefront on their minds. Those itching to get moving were asked to be patient and those feeling nervous were encouraged to be brave. During the safety brief, we were warned about the dangers, including collisions and overturns, then asked to sign disclaimer forms in case of injury or death! These formalities focused our attention as each participant took notice of how best to safely operate their 250cc vehicle. The quad bikes were parked nearby and as we each picked one, the guides did the rounds, checking that we knew how to steer, stop, and accelerate.

With engines running and the sun rising to our right, we formed a single file behind the main guide, then crossed over a palm-tree lined road towards the edge of the desert. One guide stayed at the rear, to ensure there were no stragglers, while the others stayed alert for those that needed attention. Initially, the pace was steady, so that each of us could get used to the gears, brakes and steering. This all changed as we came to a long stretch of hardened sand, flanked by gentle dunes. Our guides waved us down and offered us the chance to test out the machines and our capabilities.

One by one we raced into the desert, with a comfortable gap between each excited rider. When my turn came, I looked ahead at the dust cloud kicked up by the previous riders. Suddenly, I felt like a kid in a toy shop. Before me lay a natural playground, with no road signs, traffic lights, roundabouts, or speed cameras.

The guide gave the signal, and I didn't hesitate. As the wheels tore across the sand, I gripped the steering tight and racked through the gears. The dunes on either side blurred past as I followed in the tracks of those before me. I could have stayed that way forever, as the wind whipped against my grinning face, but far ahead I noticed a line of quad bikes, lining the edge of a dune. A guide waved me down before turning his attention to the next rider approaching. Until at last, we were all safely parked.

Throughout the morning, we enjoyed a myriad of experiences, from riding fast to taking it slow and steady while traversing along the top of vast dunes, with no end in sight of the rippling sand. At times we were warned about steep inclines, which would tip our vehicles or instructed to leisurely follow our guides in close formation, to minimise the impact on the environment. We never encountered any other groups of quad bikers, and there were no roads. It was just us, the golden dunes, and the sun, forever shining and getting stronger by the hour.

By mid-morning, we were parked at the base of a 30-metre dune. One guide pointed out the best line of attack for getting safely to the pinnacle, before heading off on a solo mission to the top. He then dismounted and walked to the far side of the ridge, to check that all was clear. Once happy, he then waved us forward one by one. Each of us rode as fast as we dared, hoping to catch some air before landing on the other side. Our guides encouraged us to complete the circuit a few more times and, on each occasion, we got braver and faster. They then led us to a half-pipe of hardened sand, ten metres high and fifty metres wide. It looked like a giant wave about to break onto a beach, and we watched as one of the guides sped towards the far edge, then turned slightly to ride fast across the steep side.

For those of us willing to try, we were warned to keep our speed up the whole time, or else we'd tumble from the half-pipe into the sand below. I watched the most experienced in our group go first and as each one returned, grinning and asking for more, I decided to give it a go. Fran was nearby, her cheeks dusty and her face a little concerned as she declined the offer of tackling the half-pipe. She watched as I revved hard and set my sights on the giant wave of sand.

The next minute flew past, as I squeezed the accelerator and set my sights on the point where I needed to commit to the turn. For a fleeting moment, my world turned sideways as I raced across the hardened face of sand, no longer grinning, but totally focused on speed and keeping a straight line. I returned to the group and gave Fran the thumbs up, while waiting in line for another attempt!

To finish the tour, we were led to a prominent ridge of dunes, each with a bird's-eye view of the surrounding terrain. Far below, the cool grey mass of the Atlantic silently pushed against the sides of the impenetrable Namib Desert; two opposing forces, locked in daily battle.

After three nights in Swakopmund, it was time to close the gap on Cape Town. Once again, we headed in a southerly direction, along a desert road devoid of towns or villages. We stopped once, at a windblown settlement, for the chance to stretch our legs, top up on water and hunt for snacks on the sandy shelves of a lonely convenience store.

The sun was low by the time we parked alongside Dune 45, a 130-metre pinnacle of sand, located in an area known as Sossusvlei. This vast, semi-arid land is home to the princes of the desert, known as gemsbok. These majestic antelope have adapted to the harsh climate and roam the desert with mysterious ease. A few stood nearby, but effortlessly remained one step ahead as each passenger made their way towards the base of Dune 45.

Our aim was to plough through the soft, red sand, to reach the summit before sunset. Some raced ahead and others stopped often, to take a breath while posing for photos. I went in search of fog basking beetles and found a few of them lining the ridge, patiently waiting for the evening mist to arrive. The precious moisture is collected in ripples on their backs and funnelled towards their mouths.

By the time I reached the top, Fran was seated alongside Wayne and Naomi. Together, we sat side by side on the sand, silently appreciating the panoramic view. Ours was not the biggest dune. The summit revealed a rippling carpet of sand stretching to the horizon, carved by searing winds and forever changing over time. Each dune differed in some way. Some were sheer-sided and lost in shadow, while others sparkled from the blaze of the setting sun.

A group of girls from our truck appeared soon after, breathless but happy. Instead of taking a rest, they joined hands and leapt over the edge, sending their excited screams across the desert as they tumbled towards the bottom. Without warning, Fran followed suit, hurtling down the angled sides and sinking into the velvety sand with each giant step. Wayne attempted to reach the desert floor in ten huge strides. I raced Naomi to the bottom, her little legs sending her spiralling into the soft sand.

We camped that night in the desert and woke to a fiery sunrise. While waiting for coffee to brew, I reached for more layers and complained about the bitter cold of the night. Tony smiled and pointed to the rising sun, before reminding me that we were in for a scorcher.

During breakfast, Jeff explained that we were close to the Spergebiet; known as the 'forbidden zone.' This vast area was once off limits to visitors for more than a century, following the discovery of diamonds. The first recorded finding occurred in 1908, by a Namibian railway worker called Zacharias Lewala. Within weeks, many more were found. Word soon spread about the field of diamonds, millions of years old, deposited by ancient sea storms onto the coast of Namibia.

At the time, the German Empire occupied most of southwest Africa, and to control the diamonds, they closed off an area of 10,000 square miles. With so many people flocking to the region, a tiny community by the name of Kolmanskop was developed into a bustling town, complete with a school, casino, skittle alley and hospital. It even had its own lemonade factory and was once regarded as the wealthiest town in the world. Kolmanskop prospered for many years until the diamonds became too difficult and costly to find.

In the 1950s, when word spread about another find, far more profitable and closer to the Orange River, the residents began leaving in droves. The last time that the local orchestra played was in 1954, to a small audience. Soon after, it packed away its instruments and abandoned the town, along with the remaining residents.

Kolmanskop is now a ghost town, but the forbidden zone remains intact, with harsh fines in place for those who enter without permission. Warning signs were positioned alongside the road, but many of the words and symbols had been bleached by the sun and eroded by sandstorms.

We'd gained a permit before our arrival, which gave us the freedom to explore the abandoned town. As soon as the truck stopped, each passenger bounded towards the broken-down buildings. I raced up a hardened mound of sand and gained access to the hospital via a missing window. After clambering through the gap, I emerged unscathed into an empty ward. The floors were covered in sand, with deep piles in each corner. Remnants of faded wallpaper clung to blistered plaster and one of the adjacent rooms contained a bathtub, now half filled with sand, blown in through a gap in the wall.

Fran appeared on the scene and took a photo while I lay in the bath, feeling the warmth of the sand as I gazed at a cloudless sky through a hole in the roof. It was hard to imagine that such a remote and dry location once had the luxury of running water and bathing facilities.

We then tried our luck in another building. Like most others, the doorframes had warped over time. I squeezed through the gap of a splintered doorway, shining my torch into an abandoned bedroom. The roof was still intact, but the windows were sealed by sand, with no sign of life in the shadows. With each breath of wind, the desert was slowly taking over the town, one grain of sand at a time.

The bus was strangely silent as we pulled away from Kolmanskop. Like most passengers, my thoughts were consumed by the once purposeful town, now abandoned and left to the mercy of the elements.

We camped by the rocky coast, on a windswept jut of land known as Shark Island. What the narrow peninsula lacked in greenery it made up for with expansive views of the grey Atlantic and glimpses of the colourful town of Luderitz, close by. After the tents had been erected, Jeff pointed towards a rocky outcrop and explained that some housed memorials to German military officers that had served in the South West Africa campaign.

While we strolled into town for a place to eat, he continued with the history lesson by explaining the chequered past of the island. Between 1905 and 1907, it was used as a concentration camp by the German authorities, to imprison members of the Heroro and Nama tribes. A year earlier, they'd rebelled against colonisation by the Germans and had paid a high price. The German high command sent out an order to shoot every Heroro found within the border. The result was near annihilation for the Heroro and Nama tribes.

Historians now regard this act as the first genocide of the 20th century. Shark Island became known as *Death Island,* as very few prisoners survived their time in the prison. Namibia, it seemed, was a country of contrasts, like so many in Africa. On one hand, it was blessed with immense beauty, but also had a dark, turbulent past, hidden away.

We were soon walking alongside the colourful art deco buildings of Luderitz. Apart from the ocean views and rows of palm trees, we could have been in a Bavarian village. The high street shops included a family-run bakery, its shop window displaying triple-decker sponge cakes, oozing with fresh cream.

Many shop names were in German, including the banks and restaurants. Throughout the afternoon walk, one building continually caught my eye. Perched high on a granite outcrop, on the edge of town, stood a stone church. Its elongated clock tower stood proudly over the rooftops, reminding us all that it was time to eat!

I woke the next morning and stepped outside my tent, expecting to gaze over the ocean. Instead, I reached for a jumper and peered through a blanket of sea mist, in search of the truck. Jeff and Tony were already awake, and while we enjoyed coffee together, the mist melted away, as the sun made an appearance and the camp came to life. It was time to prepare for the long drive south, towards the South African border.

Our last night in Namibia coincided with our final sleep in a tent. The setting was perfect, with jaw dropping views of Fish River Canyon. This huge scar on the land is second only to the Grand Canyon in size and the numbers are impressive. Even from our ideal vantage point it was hard to comprehend that the canyon is over 100 kilometres long, 27 kilometres wide and nearly a kilometre deep. With daytime temperatures in mid-summer reaching 40 degrees Celsius, the canyon can be a dangerous place. Walking tours are offered, but the scale of the area means that to fully appreciate the gorge you need to get into its belly and walk along the river. Such a feat would take days, and we only had a few hours left in Namibia.

Instead, we watched the rocks turn red, cracked open a few beers, and toasted the memorable times we'd enjoyed in Namibia. Sitting by the edge of the canyon, sharing jokes with Wayne while the sky turned dark, it was difficult to fathom that our time on the truck was ending. Within 24 hours, it would all be over.

The following day, after an easy passage through the border, the truck continued non-stop for many hours, with all eyes searching for Table Mountain. Just before sunset, its anvil shape appeared on the horizon, triggering a round of cheers from the passengers. The expedition was over.

Fran and Naomi

A quiet moment

Bath time in Kolmanskop

Dune 45

Brand New Friend

"After climbing a great hill, one only finds that there are many more hills to climb."
Nelson Mandela

The following day, we celebrated in style, by visiting the Stellenbosch wineries on an organised tour. By sunset we met again, for a spirited pub-crawl along the Victoria and Alfred waterfront. We were spoilt for choice, with an endless number of bars, cafes, shops and restaurants vying for our attention by the water's edge. The scene was dominated by Table Mountain, its flattened summit looming over the city. Just after midnight, email addresses and phone numbers were exchanged, with drunken promises to stay in touch. One by one the passengers dispersed into the balmy African night.

I woke early, to the sound of the truck kicking into life and made a dash for the curtains. In that fleeting moment, I caught sight of Jeff, Tony, and his wife, driving out of the car park. Their next passengers were probably at 35,000 feet, flying to Cape Town from far-flung parts of the globe. Who would they be this time? Maybe it would be secretaries searching for adventure, or lawyers looking for love. It could even be electricians eager to change their lives, rather than light bulbs. With Jeff in charge and Tony at the wheel, they were in excellent hands.

The breakfast bar was eerily quiet as I ordered coffee and studied the menu. Some passengers were still in bed and others were already in transit to their next destination. We decided to stay in Cape Town with Wayne and Naomi to explore the city. Our hostel was situated in the densely populated suburb of Sea Point, which had once been classified as a "whites only" area during the apartheid era. It is now a melting pot of cultures, colours, and religions.

By day we felt comfortable, but by nightfall the joviality was replaced with raised voices and altercations. During a fracas between drunken youths, we escaped the scene and dived into a corner pub. Most clientele were white and elderly, seated quietly while sipping drinks. While seated at the bar, we soon learned that the white-washed building had once been an inclusive club, for ex-pats.

I felt a tinge of sadness as we studied the worn faces, red noses and grey moustaches of the men. Most of the women wore summer dresses and cradled matching handbags. They spoke quietly and eloquently, while sipping gin and tonics. With nowhere left to go, they met here most days, watched over by a portrait of the Queen.

The scene outside was very different, with shouts and obscenities from bored teenagers as they roamed the dark streets. We returned the following night, now greeted as friends, and shared stories over drinks. They spoke of corruption, apartheid, cocktail parties, lost opportunities, hunting trips and the good old days. We spoke about travelling, adventure and the chance to live in Australia.

We woke to another blue sky and made plans to take a coastal hike, followed by an invigorating dip in the ocean, with penguins! Cape Point lies at the southern edge of Table Mountain National Park, where rugged cliffs give way to secluded beaches. Our aim was to walk to a lookout point, to view the Cape of Good Hope. This rocky headland juts proudly from the shoreline, marking the spot where sailors heading down the southwest coast of Africa can finally make a purposeful turn, as they approach the most southern part of the continent, known as Cape Agulhas.

As we parked our hired car, Naomi commented on the multitude of warning signs for wild baboons. We dismissed their importance, lured into a false sense of security by ice cream vans and excited children. We soon escaped from the crowds, as a set of sandstone steps led us away from the noise of cars and people.

Earlier, we'd read about the abundance of wildlife found within the national park, but as we strode purposefully along a coastal track, there was no sign of zebras within the pockets of greenery, or baboons studying us from rocky outcrops. Ostriches also survive in the coastal heath, but they also proved elusive. Instead of searching for wild animals, we turned our attention to the deep waters of False Bay, where sailing boats jostled for position between the swells. An hour later, while enjoying snacks and water, we sat on a grassy bank to enjoy the faraway sight of a rocky outcrop–which we all agreed–had to be the Cape of Good Hope!

We returned along the same path, into a stiff wind with the sun on our weary faces. By the time we returned to the car park, all thoughts were on ice creams and refreshments. After enjoying vanilla cones sprinkled with chocolate, we crossed the tarmac towards our Ford Fiesta. It was Naomi that spotted the movement, far to our left. 'I think we're being followed,' she said, while pointing towards a mother and baby baboon, scurrying parallel to us. With inquisitive eyes, they watched as we opened the boot to stow our daypacks.

'Get in the car,' demanded Wayne. 'These things can bite.'

After we raced in, the mother jumped onto the bonnet and stared through the windscreen while we prepared to leave.

'Ali, don't muck around–just go!' ordered Wayne, as the girls shrilled with laughter at the unwanted visitor. Ignoring Wayne's instructions, I was eager for fun and decided to turn the dial for the windscreen wipers. After calling for attention, I flicked the switch. Instead of the swishing of wipers, the only sound we heard was a dull click, as the car boot sprung open. From the rear seats, Wayne's booming voice was impossible to miss. 'You idiot. You've pushed the wrong button!'

The boot lid was fully open, exposing all our possessions and luggage. The baboon bolted over the roof and onto the tarmac. It landed alongside the open boot, prompting Wayne to call out. 'Our passports are in that bag! Toe it–now!'

I wanted to explain that the hired car had different switches than the type I normally drove in the UK, but knew the best thing was to speed up, with no explanation. We squealed out of the car park, with the mother in pursuit. The road turned sharply at an intersection and I yanked on the wheel. A small bundle of fur whizzed off the roof, past Fran's window. Now we knew where the baby had been hiding! It rolled across the grass and shook itself off, before jumping onto the back of its mother. Together, they boldly headed off, in search of more tourists.

Despite the giggles from the girls, Wayne continued his rant. 'You silly pommy bastard. Stop the car round the next corner and shut the boot!'

The girls asked him to calm, as I pulled over to the side of the road and got out to close the boot. Returning to my seat I winked at Naomi and turned my attention to Wayne. 'I think your rucksack must be at the hostel as it's not in the boot.'

He held my gaze and eased out a smile. 'Ali, you're either a comedian or a bloody liar. Let's get going, it's nearly beer o'clock.'

I'd just found my first Australian friend! An hour later, we were in Boulders Bay and all was forgiven. We were dressed in bathers, while gasping from the cool ocean spray. Wayne went in first and we followed soon after. Although cold, the water was crystal clear, with feisty waves that broke onto the golden shoreline. We swam into deeper waters and were soon rewarded with the sighting of African penguins. They were dark and fast in the water and rarely came close.

The following day we headed for the shantytowns, on one of the many organised tours that allow tourists a safe visit to these significant areas. In the early afternoon, we entered Khayelitsha, one of the fastest growing townships in Cape Town. This is where we met Vicky. She'd had the vision to open a bed-and-breakfast, in an area where travellers receive stern warnings never to enter alone. By involving the local community, she has brought a small piece of prosperity and a sense of dignity to this run-down neighbourhood.

Vicky wore colourful clothes and kept her hair in a frizz. She also had an infectious, hearty laugh, but underneath the makeup I sensed a proud woman, with an inner strength. As with most houses in the crowded street, the exterior was clad with corrugated iron and salvaged wood. The interior looked far homelier, with brightly coloured décor and family photos on display. There were cards and thank you messages from across the world, sent by visitors that had enjoyed their experience. We booked to stay for the night and were shown to our bedroom. While Fran tried out the bed, I stood at the window to take in the view.

The square patch of garden looked dry and unkempt but had a washing line. There were no fences to distinguish where one garden finished, and another started. The washing lines of other neighbours were also on display, and the lines daisy-chained across the ramshackle gardens, where children laughed while mothers prepared food in the shade.

On the front lawn, a group of cheerful black lads stood over a barbeque, avidly watching four sheep's heads blacken, in time for dinner. I noticed a low-pitched building across the road, which Vicky explained was the local *shebeen*, or pub. In normal circumstances, going over for a few beers would not be a smart move, but she insisted we were safe if we didn't wander any further.

The decor was simple, with two pool tables and a scattering of tables and chairs. Two young men sat playing cards in the corner, looking up as Fran tentatively pushed open the mesh door. I stood alongside her and called out, 'Hi there. Vicky sent us over to challenge you at pool.'

They both smiled as we stepped inside. The barman was partially hidden behind an iron grille and passed cold beers through one of the gaps. I handed two bottles to the men and grabbed a pool cue. We left half an hour later, easily beaten at pool, with high fives all round.

Our next stop was a girls-only school, which had been hand built by the local community, using donated bricks. The rough walls were decorated with colourful hand-drawn pictures and the teacher had a simple wooden desk at the front, along with a blackboard. Each pupil sat obediently, while their teacher introduced the overseas visitors. The schoolgirls were dressed immaculately, in white blouses and matching skirts. The teacher briefly informed us about the charities that provide the clothes, lunchtime snacks, and school equipment. She then invited us all into a courtyard, where the girls stood together and began singing. It didn't take long before Fran was alongside, clapping and dancing to their soulful tune.

Pre-judged expectations of life in shantytowns were fading, but our tour guide grounded my optimism during the next excursion. He pulled the minivan over to the side of the road, getting us to line up along the verge, and pointed to a vast area that glistened with tin roofs. 'Over there, is a township called Crossroads.'

He then turned to face us and waited for silence. 'It is a dangerous town and your safety is not guaranteed in such a place. It is sad for me, as many people who live there are decent people. But gangs roam the streets of Crossroads. They are poor, and most will never get the chance to travel. They have little schooling and few prospects, which can make them envious of outsiders. I hope you are learning something today, my friends. Please grab some water, as I have more to tell you.'

While standing on the dusty roadside, we learnt the differences between blacks, coloureds and whites and their respective subcultures. Then he tried explaining how the melting pot of religions and tribes manage to live side by side, despite their differences. His final words were about the decades of apartheid that had divided the country and the emotional scars that would take many years to heal. It seemed to me that South Africa was a complicated place to fully understand.

By sunset, we were back in our simple hostel and began packing for our overnight stay in the shantytown. Partway through, we received a message that Vicky's driver had broken down on the way to collect us. After all that we had learnt, it felt risky to order a taxi to take us there. With few streetlights, an unfamiliar neighbourhood and a high crime rate to consider, we reluctantly unpacked our clothes and decided to stay put.

The following morning, we boarded a local ferry, along with many other excited tourists, for a 30-minute trip across Table Bay. Our destination was Robben Island, a low-lying, oval-shaped parcel of land, approximately three kilometres long and two kilometres wide. It is home to thousands of birds, including African penguins and its coastal waters teem with life.

Despite the isolation and rugged beauty, the island was once a place of oppression and heartache. For centuries, some of those from the mainland that were regarded as criminals or outcasts became exiled on the island. The prison that once held Nelson Mandela still stands on the island and is now a major tourist attraction. Because of the historical significance of the prison and associated buildings, UNESCO has classified the island as a World Heritage Site.

Our guide was a former inmate and after a warm welcome soon began crafting dark tales of life and death in the sprawling prison. The intimate tour included a visit to a nearby quarry, where inmates would often spend hours in the sun, breaking rocks with sledgehammers. The guide then led us to the wing that once held Nelson Mandela. Most onlookers jostled for space outside his cramped cell, as the guide explained the strict rules and regulations that Mandela and his fellow inmates had to follow each day.

I tried taking a photo of the steel bars that once held him, but was nudged aside by an eager tourist. Instead of competing with the crowd, I drifted to the back and took in the scene. I was standing on a polished floor, with rows of cells along one side. I had no idea of the names of those that were once imprisoned in them, except for Nelson Mandela. I also knew very little about the reasons for their incarceration. The guide was trying to explain, but our group was too large, and I didn't feel like barging to the front.

An hour later, we crossed a courtyard on the way to view the kitchens. To my right, I recognised a door that we'd been through earlier. It was the entrance to Mandela's cellblock. I pulled Fran to one side and quickly explained. 'Keep with the guide, as I'm going back.'

I sprinted across the exposed courtyard and tried the door, expecting it to be locked. It nudged open and I stepped inside without a backward glance. My heart began racing at the thought of getting caught. But I wasn't doing anything wrong. I was just after a piece of solitude. The only sound was my soft footsteps as I strolled along the corridor towards Mandela's empty cell. I ran my hands along the polished bars and then sat for a while outside his former cell. I closed my eyes for a few moments, yearning to know the whispered conversations of the interned, but time and emulsion had erased all scent of the former inmates.

Weeks later, I investigated his time at the prison and came across a statement he made after his release. "Never, never and never again shall it be that this beautiful land will again experience the oppression of one by another."

The trip to the island had lifted my spirits, showing once again that we all have choices in how we act, when faced with formidable challenges. Mandela refused to be beaten by oppression, despite the odds stacked against him!

Our final evening in Cape Town was spent on the summit of Table Mountain. We could have trekked to the top, but decided to take the cable car instead. We'd packed wine, cheese and crackers and soon found a suitable spot to watch the sun turn red and fall slowly from the sky. While Wayne poured drinks and Fran prepared snacks, Naomi pointed towards a layer of mist, creeping across the anvil summit, like dry ice at the theatre. But this wasn't make-believe. We were on top of one of the most iconic mountains in the world, with panoramic views of the city far below, fringed by the deep waters of Table Bay.

As we watched, the city seemed to come to life, as thousands of bright dots gave away the position of cars, houses, hotel rooms, streetlights, and shantytowns. The urban sprawl looked to be held back by a swathe of greenery, which was now turning dark as the sun dipped below the waterline. The national park that blankets the lower slopes of the mountain was once home to cape lions and leopards, but they are no longer found in the reserve. Botanists are in their element though, with thousands of species of flora thriving in the Mediterranean climate.

As we huddled together with Wayne and Naomi, the moment felt right to share our dreams and aspirations. Their goals were set, with job interviews in Australia already in motion. Naomi leaned nearer, flushed from the local wine. 'Hey guys, come and live in Perth. We can be your mates.'

I looked over at Fran and said, 'Well, there's an offer you don't hear every day.'

In reply, Wayne eased out a smile while mumbling from the rocky outcrop. 'I hope you won't be whinging Poms.'

I returned his smile and hugged Fran close. Our future was still uncertain, but for now we could sit together and enjoy the last of the sunset.

We woke to another fine day and made plans to depart the city in our hired car. Our destination was the coastal town of Knysna, 500 kilometres east of Cape Town. The journey would take us through the Garden Route, a diverse parcel of land that is sandwiched between the ocean and the mountains. Weekenders, honeymooners, wine tour enthusiasts, thrill seekers and sun worshipers are all attracted to the coastal strip, as it has something for everyone. Quaint fishing villages and picture-perfect beaches call for your attention, as does the chance to explore the nearby forests. Those looking for adventure can try their luck at rock-climbing, deep-sea fishing or cage diving with great white sharks!

During the next few days we enjoyed cream teas in seaside towns, joined a wine tour with a group of backpackers and hired mountain bikes, to explore the wooded hills. By the time we reached the seaside town of Knysna, our time with Wayne and Naomi was nearly over, with both parties preparing to go their separate ways. They were staying put for a while longer and we needed to be at Johannesburg airport within a few days. Fran was due to fly to Romania and my flight was booked for Sydney. With luck, we'd meet with them again, somewhere in Australia.

With one more night left together, we made plans to eat in a beachside restaurant, to celebrate our adventures in Africa. Before heading out, I packed my bag and advised Fran to do the same, as we wouldn't be returning to the hostel. Instead, we were booked on a midnight shuttle bus to take us inland. Fran was not as excited as me to be heading to Zululand on an overnight bus, but as she completed her packing, I explained my reasons for wanting to visit the area.

My fascination with Zululand had been sparked years earlier, while reading a story by the novelist, Wilbur Smith, describing the

Zulu tribes fighting for their independence during the Anglo-Zulu War of 1879. The book conjured up images of a majestic and savage landscape, filled with vast tracts of grassland, dotted with green hills and forests. Those battling for survival in this unforgiving place included wild animals, ancient tribes, hunters, soldiers, and settlers.

It isn't only his books that had fuelled my enthusiasm for the Anglo-Zulu War. Michael Caine once starred in a blockbuster movie called *Zulu*, about a long and bloody battle that took place at a remote outpost, called Rorke's Drift. After watching the film many times, I could recite each dramatic event, line by line. Now, I was finally in reach of the actual location. With bags packed and bus tickets stored safely away, we strolled into town during the last of the light. Along the way, we stopped at intervals to admire the picket-fenced houses overlooking an expansive lagoon, dotted with islands and bordered by sandstone cliffs. Beyond the headland, lay the Indian Ocean, fed by the wide waters of the Knysna River.

Sometime later, the girls were dancing on stage with a local rock band and I was sitting by the bar, alongside Wayne. The barman suggested a few local drinks and we didn't refuse. Just before midnight, we raised our glasses high and promised to meet again in Australia. Soon after, while holding takeaway kebabs, I steered Fran towards the waiting bus. Once on board, we tearfully waved to Wayne and Naomi through the steamed-up windows and settled down for the long journey ahead.

I woke six hours later and opened my eyes. I was lying in the aisle, with a jacket by my side. All I could see were dozens of feet from other passengers and the scrunched-up paper from the earlier takeaway. No one seemed to notice as I stood and stretched, then made my way towards Fran, a few seats away. She was curled up asleep; her face hidden beneath a jumper. After too many hours and two more bus trips, we arrived on the fringes of Zululand, near the historic monument of Fort Mistake.

Located on top of a rounded hill, this once vital garrison was used for communication between the major towns of Ladysmith and Newcastle during the Anglo-Boer war. The base of the hill was to be our pickup point for one of the many guides who make their living by giving tours of the battlefields, which are spread throughout the Natal Province of South Africa.

As arranged, we were met by Dave, our tour guide. He was a tall, overweight man, with a shock of brown hair and weathered face. But as he reached for Fran's heavy rucksack, his smile seemed as warm as the afternoon sun on our backs. After such a long journey, we were eager for some creature comforts and happily sat in his minibus as he drove to a nearby hotel, aptly called the Battlefields Country Lodge.

With a promise to return in the morning, he left us to enjoy a night of comfort. With a pool, restaurant, bar and spacious bedroom, the accommodation seemed perfect. Just before sunset I made my way to the reception desk, in search of a place to enjoy sundowners with Fran. While in the lobby, I picked up a flyer, welcoming me to the heartland of the historic battlefields of KwaZulu Natal.

Further information revealed that the hotel overlooked, *the famous Talana Hill.* After venturing onto the manicured lawn, I gazed across the surrounding grassland in search of the hill. Nearby, a hotel guest lounged in a comfy chair and watched with interest as I peered at the undulating terrain. Like many other male guests that I'd seen that afternoon, he was grey-haired and sported a grand moustache. He got to his feet and pointed to a low-lying, flat-topped hill. 'Are you searching for Talana Hill? They say it's worth the climb, but I'm guessing it wouldn't have been quite so pleasant in October 1899.'

I stared back blankly as he briefly explained that the hill had once been the focal point for the first major clash of the Second Boer War. Just as he began to get into the gory details about the bloody battle, his wife appeared, dressed for dinner in a floral dress. After she'd ushered him away with an apology, I stared once more at the sunburnt hill, suddenly aware that I knew very little about the history of the area.

Two hours later, while seated with Fran at the bar, I spotted someone waving to gain our attention. It was the woman that I'd met on the lawn. She was seated with her husband and as our eyes met, she called out, 'Hello again. Are you both in the services? Would you like to join us for a nightcap? We went on a battlefields tour today, didn't we Eric?'

As we got up from our seats, her husband smiled and raised his whisky glass. But we were in no mood for chitchat, as the long journey from Knysna had finally taken its toll. While passing their table, we stopped briefly to say goodnight. Once again, she asked if we were in the military. I stifled a yawn, happy to let Fran do the talking. 'No, we're not in the military, but do enjoy travelling. Yesterday, we were in Knysna, 14 hours away. We're here because my husband loves a film called Zulu and has read lots of books by Wilbur Smith. Thanks so much for the offer of a drink, but we really need to sleep. Within two days, I'll be on my way to Romania, which is currently covered in snow and ice.'

She then turned towards me and said, 'My husband, on the other hand, is off to Sydney, Australia. While he'll be basking in sunshine on Bondi Beach, I'll be rugged up in thermals and a woollen hat, traipsing the frozen streets in search of a police officer to bribe!'

And with that, she nudged me into action, as we waved goodbye to the watching couple and headed to our first decent bed in weeks.

The following morning, after a dip in the pool, followed by a leisurely breakfast, we met with Dave once again. He welcomed us on board his minivan and asked us to pick any seat we wanted. Most other passengers looked to be in their fifties or sixties and seemed to know each other by name. We made our way to the back, settled into the rear seats and fiddled with a vent in the hope of getting some air.

As soon as we were on the road, an overhead speaker crackled to life as Dave gave a few taps on the microphone. After a warm welcome, he began the journey with a history lesson about the British invasion of Zululand in 1879. Sometime later, diamonds were mentioned, as well as colonial expansion, greed, Boer fighters and the Dutch. We nodded politely, sipped on water and stared out of the windows at the rolling green hills, far in the distance.

Our first stop was Isandlwana, an isolated hill where the British army suffered their single largest defeat at the hands of a native army, with thousands killed. While Dave spoke, my eyes were drawn to a granite crag that dominated the top of the steep incline. I'd liked to have trekked to the top, but all too soon, we were on the road again.

Unfortunately, his itinerary didn't include any stopovers at Zulu communities. I didn't expect to see bands of warriors at each hilltop banging on leopard skin shields, but was still hoping for a chance to meet some locals. Ideally, we'd have stopped in a village, enjoyed a meal and got the chance to mingle with those who lived and worked nearby. But we drove past each village, towards the sites of smaller, long forgotten, battles. Fran's eyes began to droop as the hours passed and the passionate guide retold each escapade with intimate detail.

By late afternoon, we pulled into our final destination, Rorke's Drift, where 139 British troops and 11 colonial soldiers managed, against all odds, to defend the mission station against 4,000 Zulu warriors. The manicured grounds and neat buildings masked the past atrocities, although a lack of visitors gave us the opportunity to explore the serene outpost. As the sun cast long shadows across the valley, our guide began his last speech. With each new sentence, the pitch of his voice slowly intensified.

While he spoke about fear, courage, death, and bravery, I stepped away from the group to find some solitude. I walked alongside the field hospital and began striding up the nearby hill. The coarse grass was ankle high and the earth felt spongy from recent rains. The smell of wood smoke caught in my throat, drifting from a nearby settlement. By the time I stopped to admire the view, I was panting for breath. From up high, I had a commanding view of the garrison nestled in the quiet valley. I knelt to touch the earth, trying to imagine the noise as thousands of brave barefoot warriors surged towards the thin red line of troops. As they approached, there would have been an order to open fire, signalling the beginning of the battle.

At 100 yards, volley fire, present. Aim. Fire!

The sky had changed colour now. There was no longer any blue and our time in Africa was nearly over. After another night in the same bed, we enjoyed the chance to laze away the morning in the pool. By early afternoon, we were on board a shuttle bus to Johannesburg, 500 kilometres away. Unfortunately, a tyre change by the side of the road, followed by a bout of engine trouble, added many hours to our journey.

While the bus was being repaired, I asked Fran if she thought I should join her in Romania, as there was still time to buy an airfare ticket. In reply, she set the scene for what lay ahead. 'Ali, I speak the language and have friends there to help. I checked earlier, and there has been lots of snow. I can get a loan of warm clothes and hopefully be in and out of the country within a week. Plus, there's the additional cost of another flight.'

I didn't put up an argument. How could I, with thoughts of warm sunny days in Sydney, hard to push away. By the time we arrived on the outskirts of the city, the sky was dark. The bus pulled into a sparsely lit bus station, allowing the passengers to disperse quickly and quietly. Within minutes, they'd vanished into the night. A scattering of waiting passengers stood expectantly on the concrete platform for the next shuttle bus. They watched as we made our way to the driver, who was locking up the bus.

'Excuse me, but where is the best place to get a taxi?' I asked.

He pointed to the silhouette of two cars, parked at the edge of the station. 'See over there. That is the taxi rank. But be careful in Joburg at night, as it can be a dangerous place.'

'How much should we pay for a lift to the airport hostel?'

He looked us over, studied our luggage and pondered the question. 'Do not pay more than 20 dollars. They will ask for more, but I'm sure you know that. Good luck and goodnight.'

With that, he pocketed the key and walked away. The young drivers perched on the rusted bonnet of the first car watched as we approached. I cleared my throat and called out confidently. 'Good evening, we need to get to the airport hostel. Can you take us, please?'

One driver leapt from the bonnet, skidding to a halt on the oil-stained roadside. His training shoes were a brilliant white, in stark contrast to his matted jeans, which struggled to stay tight on his limp body. He smiled briefly, revealing gleaming white teeth, in need of flossing. Fran's overladen rucksack was scooped up easily. 'Of course I can help you. It's my job,' he announced proudly.

'That's great. How much will that be, please?'

Fran's bag was now on his back, ready to be placed into the boot, but he stopped and smiled again. 'The price is 60 dollars. It's a special price because it is quiet tonight.'

My stomach turned. 'Sorry, mate, but the bus driver told us it would be about 20.'

The bag thudded onto the floor and he moved nearer. 'What does the bus driver know about taxi prices? Have a think about that while I go for a walk.'

Joined by his friend, he strutted away from the bus station, leaving us alone by the isolated taxis. We instinctively followed him as he strode away. All we wanted was a bed for the night, and I was keen to end the charade. This eagerness took us away from the relative safety of the station, towards an underground pass.

The driver turned to face us and called out, 'Okay, I will lower my price to 50 dollars.' He then returned to his friend before we could reply. A small crowd of youths gathered closer to listen to the negotiations, which prompted me to study our surroundings. There were few streetlights, hardly any traffic, and no pedestrians. I caught the whiff of urine and finally took notice of the broken bottles strewn across the tarmac.

An argument was taking place near the underpass, with obscenities being traded between two youths. Then there were more shouts and the beginnings of a scuffle. A young lad raced from the shadows and pushed an abandoned shopping trolley into the path of a speeding car. The vehicle veered away and squealed into the humid night. It was also time to make a hasty departure! I turned to Fran and lowered my voice. 'We need to get in the taxi right now. Don't worry about the fare, we'll sort it out on the way.'

The driver joined us within seconds, started up the car and turned to confirm the price. His smile had returned, but his narrow eyes told another story. I should have agreed with his fee, but for some reason still felt compelled to get a lower price. He replied in an instant through gritted teeth. 'Why do rich people always haggle?'

Fran squeezed my arm tightly, to bring me to my senses. While I gathered my thoughts, the driver had the last word. 'My final price is 40 dollars. Accept the price or look for another taxi.'

My eyes darted to the remaining taxi driver, who was now lying flat on his back on the bonnet of his car. 'Okay, 40 dollars sounds like a deal. Can we go now, please?'

He screeched away from the kerb, clipped the upturned trolley and sped into the night. Fran released her grip on my sweaty arm and whispered about the stifling heat in the back. In response, I started to wind down the nearest window. The rush of air brought instant relief, followed by the sound of cursing from our driver. He turned in his seat, calling out loud. 'What the hell are you doing? That window is broken and doesn't wind up. Why did you touch it? This is not my car. My boss will make me pay.'

While Fran sat silently beside me, I tried to calm the situation. 'Look, I'm sorry. It's hot in the back and we just needed to cool down. I'll fix it or pay for it.'

'Yes, you will,' he demanded, before speeding off once again. A warm blast of air roared through the interior of the car, as he hurtled past rows of abandoned shops. Shutters were smeared with graffiti and groups of youths stood idle at each corner. I knelt close to the handle and tried winding it up. Although the worn gears clunked and slipped with each grinding revolution, the window slowly inched higher. With a sense of relief, I finally sealed the gap. The noise subsided in an instant, which returned the taxi to an awkward silence.

The streets outside looked dark and deserted, with few cars on the road. My mind was racing with morbid thoughts and Fran's hand was once again squeezing my arm. Up ahead, I noticed a streetlight, followed by the sight of a corner store, still open despite the late hour. Brightly lit cafés appeared, along with city-goers in search of entertainment or food. Fran eased her fingers from my arm, allowing blood to return as we joined a long queue of slow-moving traffic. Our driver mumbled inconsistently, either lost in thought or attempting to convey a message.

We ignored the ramblings and turned our attention to the passing street life. Within two sharp turns we were alone again, driving through a vast industrial estate, past lonely car parks and empty paddocks. While I studied the road for signs of life, our driver continually turned his attention towards us. 'My boss wants all the money. I must rent this shitty car and you have broken the window. I have nothing, and you have everything. Why do you people always try to pay so little?'

His voice suddenly rose in tempo as he let loose with a barrage of threats. 'Do you know what I should do? I should rob you. It's much more profitable. I have no money and I hate my job.'

In that moment, my senses sharpened. This could spiral out of control, and we needed to be prepared. The airport had to be close by, but it seemed to me that the driver was contemplating his next move. While we sat quietly in the back, he continued to rant and rave as the car headlights shone ahead on a lonely road.

As his threats intensified, I reached in the dark for a Swiss Army knife, which lay somewhere in the depths of my rucksack. It was a wedding present from our friend, Paul. Why he thought we needed an army knife rather than a toaster was lost on us at the time. While scrambling round in a bag full of smelly clothes, I silently applauded his vision. I found the knife and fumbled in the dim light to release the blade.

The first device to pop out was the bottle opener. Fran looked down at the tool, her eyes struggling with the thought of fending off an attack with such a blunt instrument. The car stopped and we looked up sharply. We'd come to the end of the industrial area and were sitting at a major intersection. A huge sign illuminated the T-junction. One way pointed to the airport, the other direction would send us back into darkened suburbs. He stopped briefly, allowing a truck to pass, and pulled in behind it. A flashing sign up ahead displayed the outline of an aircraft. With a sense of relief, I placed the knife into the rucksack and squeezed Fran's hand.

Our airport hostel was located behind a security gate, but as we pulled over to park at reception, the driver began swearing once again. I silently got out and helped Fran with her backpack, then turned my attention to the scowling driver. 'I'm really sorry about the window. Please take 60 dollars.'

He took the money without a word and sped into the darkness. Despite his threats and outbursts, I felt for the driver. We were heading for Australia and further adventures; he was heading back to a deserted bus station, hoping to collect another customer.

After a night in Johannesburg, staying in a cosy hostel, it was time to go our separate ways for a few weeks. Fran boarded first, holding back tears as she prepared to touch down during the middle of a Romanian winter. Although I was heading to Australia during midsummer, I felt apprehension rather than excitement, as I settled into my window seat.

While the flight crew carried out their final checks, I stared out of the nearest window. Numerous work vehicles were in motion, all with flashing lights. Some were filled with people and others had trailers attached, stacked with cargo or equipment. Far in the distance, I noticed a long-haul passenger jet, inching away from the gate. It struck me that I could have been anywhere in the world, and yet, far beyond the control tower, lay the sprawling townships.

This was where the Vicky's of the world lived, challenging their status and carving out new lives, despite the hardships. Then there was Zululand, steeped in history and strikingly beautiful. I then cast my mind back to the splendour of Cape Town and the rugged route we'd taken through Zimbabwe, Botswana and Namibia. Where was the bright yellow overland truck now? As for Troy, we even enjoyed a few beers together during the last week of the overland trip.

I heard the engine pitch rise and checked my seatbelt once more. I felt ready to depart, but didn't want to let go of all the special memories of my travels in Africa. My mind wandered back, to when my brother, Dave, trekked ahead to Kibo hut to secure a room for us all. Within that group had been Oscar, the guide who had safely escorted me from the crater rim, along with Owen and Beryl.

Just as the plane began to taxi, I smiled widely at the thought of Captain Rastaman, standing proudly at the helm of his dhow. My thoughts then turned to the elderly tailor from Stone Town and the meticulous pride he'd shown in repairing my khaki trousers. I was wearing them now, in preparation for new adventures in Australia.

Then suddenly we were hurtling down the runway, and my face was pressed to the window. Ever so gently, the captain eased the wheels from the tarmac and my African adventure was over.

Postcards from South America:

A Pig in a Taxi, Cotopaxi and Two Sticks of Dynamite

After losing his job, Alistair takes the plunge and travels into the wilds of South America with his wife. Months later, they were running for their lives in Bolivia!

Join Alistair and Fran as they raft down the Amazon, teach English in the jungle, climb volcanoes and endure a hair-raising taxi ride across the Andes, along with a pig! Before tackling the Inca trail, they hired a donkey called Angus and trekked across a remote mountain pass, with just a mud map to guide them.

While venturing off the beaten track, they discovered Inca ruins, bustling markets and mountain villages inhabited by kindly folk offering food and shelter. If you enjoy fun-filled travel stories, *Postcards from South America* will tempt you to reach for a map, pack your bags and take the trip you've always dreamed about!

A Taste of Australia:

Bite-sized travels across a Sunburned Country

"Alone and afraid, I shook my head in astonishment and tried to sum up the situation. This had to be the most dangerous tourist attraction in Australia, yet there were no disclaimer forms to fill in–no friendly guides to offer advice–no ropes to hold on to–and no adrenaline junkies waiting in line. It was just me–halfway up the tallest climbing tree in the world–holding on for dear life!"

Renowned for its ice-cold beers, endless summers, deadly creatures and friendly locals, Alistair was keen to discover the people and places that make Australia one of the most popular travel destinations in the world. These escapades have taken him to the top of Sydney Harbour Bridge and into the searing outback, foraging for bush-tucker with an Aboriginal guide. Along the way, he's experienced the boom and bust of Kalgoorlie, where heat and dust are a way of life and everyone in town knows the price of gold. From the wilds of Tasmania to the bustling laneways of Melbourne and laid-back vibe of Perth, join Alistair as he goes in search of the *real* Australia, from deserts to the ocean, including the island of Rottnest for the chance to meet the cutest creature on planet earth.

Bring me Sunshine:

More Bite-sized Travels across a Sunburned Country

"Before us lay a road into no man's land–filled with rivers, gorges and vast tracts of open plains. Far on the horizon, a shimmering haze gave few clues to what lay beyond, as the tropical sun beat down on a parched land, begging for rain. After cranking the air conditioning, I called out a warning to the kids to watch out for crocodiles, snakes and kangaroos. We were heading into the wild!"

Join travel writer Alistair McGuinness as he embarks on more bite-sized adventures across Australia, including a campervan trip from Sydney to the hipster paradise of Byron Bay. Armed with a curious nature and a desire to enjoy each new experience, these travels also lead him into the wilds, foraging for bush tucker with an Aboriginal guide, before diving into the crystal-clear waters of Ningaloo Reef.

Each new adventure offers something different, from the vast iron ore mines of the Pilbara to the wild beauty of Monkey Mia, famed for its bottle-nosed dolphins. Along the way, Alistair encounters nomads, tourists and friendly locals, each with a tale to tell about their travels in Australia. If you enjoy travel stories, this fun-filled memoir will have you reaching for a map of Australia and planning your own adventures as you immerse yourself in the wonders of a land Down Under. With each turn of the page, you'll be transported to a place where the beers are cold, the days are sunny, and the open road stretches forever.

End to End:

John O'Groats, Broken Spokes and a Dog called Gretna

When three friends set off on a 900-mile trip to explore Britain, using an out of date map to guide them, the scene is set for a wayward adventure. One cyclist didn't own a bike, but luckily, his brother was working out of town and had one in his garage. Painted racing green, with wide wheels and a robust frame, it was far from perfect for such a trip. But it was free!

Along the way they visited numerous country pubs, went in search of the remaining Beatles, discovered an ancient hideaway used by Scottish clans, and survived a storm in the Highlands. Each time they got lost they were helped by a variety of kind and quirky characters. If you like adventure travel books, then you'll enjoy this tale about three ordinary men, proving that extraordinary things can happen, just when you least expect it. For one of the cyclists, the journey would change his life forever.

Slow Down and Enjoy the Ride

Is it possible to cycle 1,000 miles across Britain in 13 days and still find the time to slow down and enjoy the ride? Twenty years after riding from Land's End to John O'Groats, Alistair set out with his friends to repeat the adventure and quickly discovered that times have changed. Bike computers have replaced maps and thousands of cycle paths now criss-cross Britain. It didn't help that he now lives in Australia and spends more time on a paddleboard than two wheels.

With little training and a borrowed bike, he set off from Land's End, determined to enjoy every moment. Faced with so many natural distractions, he soon began deviating from the plan. With many miles to cover along remote tracks, these diversions came at a price and something had to break. Would it be the bike, the camaraderie or Alistair's inquisitive nature?

Along the way he survived heatstroke in Devon, went in search of a lady called Daphne, and braved wild storms in Glasgow. After a swim in Loch Ness, he found time to enjoy a beer in one of the remotest pubs in Scotland. Everyone who travels across Britain has a story to tell. This is Alistair's.

If you like travel books, you'll enjoy this inspirational story, which shows that with luck, curiosity and perseverance, anything is possible.

Acknowledgements

Thanks to my wife, Francine, for giving me the space and freedom to lock myself away in the study to write. She lovingly supplied tea and biscuits at all hours and added inspirational advice during those moments of doubt.

A special thank you goes to Billy Bragg for his permission to reproduce some lyrics from the iconic song, "A New England."

This book is dedicated to my younger brother, Matthew. He once packed a bag and travelled much further and far longer than I ever dared to. One day, I'd like to read about his escapades!

I enjoy keeping in touch with readers and you can find me at the following locations:

On my website @ alistairmcguinness.com

On Facebook @ alistairmcguinnesswriter

On Instagram @ alistair_mcguinness

I hope you enjoyed Wild about Africa. It has been a few years since my travels, and I yearn to return there someday. If you have a few minutes to spare, I'd really appreciate an online review.

Happy travels,

Alistair

Printed in Great Britain
by Amazon

63158622R00137